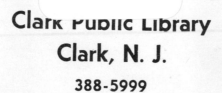

Clark Public Library
Clark, N. J.
388-5999

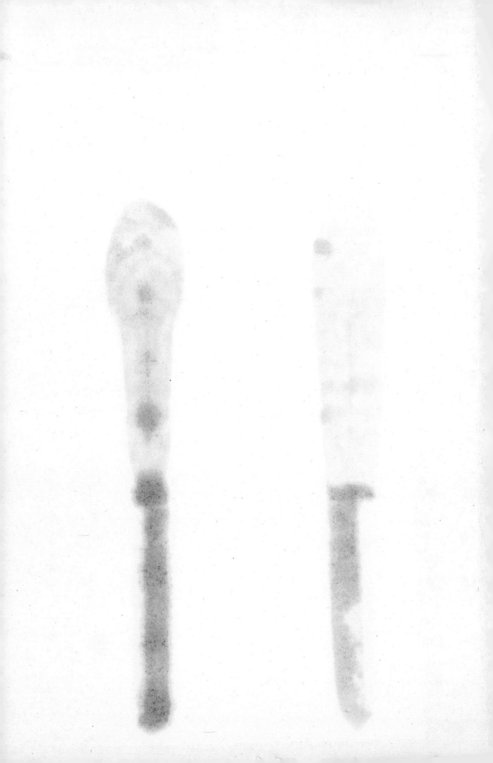

Other Lives

The Story of Reincarnation

Other Lives

*The Story of
Reincarnation by
I. G. Edmonds*

McGraw-Hill Book Company

*New York St. Louis San Francisco
Montreal Toronto*

Library of Congress Cataloging in Publication Data

Edmonds, I.G.   Other lives.
Bibliography: p.   Includes index.
Summary: Discusses reincarnation, its occurence in the
folklore of primitive people around the world, and some of
the famous people who have believed in it.
  1. Reincarnation—Juvenile literature.
 [1. Reincarnation] I. Title.
  BL515.E35   291.2'3   79–14689
  ISBN 0–07–018987–0

Contents

To the Reader

Reincarnation—the belief that the human soul can be reborn after death into a new body—is very old and very controversial. Despite centuries of arguments, neither the pros nor the cons have proven that the theory of rebirth is true or untrue.

Many famous people have believed ardently in it. Others just as famous have angrily rejected the idea. I have tried to take an informative look at the major arguments of those who believe in it. At the same time, in order to give a well-rounded view, I have included the conflicting opinions of those who are not believers. This leaves the reader to choose which side he or she wishes to believe.

The purpose of Other Lives is to provide an introduction for young people to this most fascinating subject. It is hoped that they will want to go on to a deeper and more involved study.

• I •

The Believers

When Benjamin Franklin was a young man he wrote some words that he said he wanted carved on his gravestone when he died. They were never used. But friends heard about them. For the rest of his life Franklin was often asked for a copy of what he had written.

What Franklin wrote was this:

The body of B. Franklin
Printer
Like the Covers of an Old Book
Its Contents Torn out
and
Stripped of its Lettering and Gilding
Lies Here
Food for Worms,
But the Work Shall Not be Lost
For it Will as He Believed
Appear Once More
In a New and more Elegant Edition
Revised and Corrected
By the Author.

In this amusing way Benjamin Franklin paid tribute to his work as a printer, and to his belief that death is not the end of life. Franklin believed that the human soul could be reborn after the body died, and that it would have a new life.

Ralph Waldo Emerson once quoted a letter of Franklin's in which this line is found: "I look upon death to be as necessary as sleep; we shall rise refreshed in the morning."

In another letter Franklin said that he did not believe that God would waste the millions of souls He has created. These souls would be used again. He added that despite the troubles of this life he would not object to "a new edition of mine, hoping, however, that the *errata* [mistakes] of the last may be corrected."

Benjamin Franklin, whom American history regards as a very wise man, was but one of many famous people of all ages who believed that the human soul is reborn into a new body after the old one dies.

Belief in rebirth after death seems to be as old as man himself. We find traces of this belief in the myths and legends of most primitive peoples. The belief has been found in Africa, India, China, Europe, and North America. These myths take many forms. Sometimes a great chief is reborn to lead his people in time of danger. Sometimes the tales tell of people reborn in animal form. Others speak of wicked people who returned because of great sins in other lives. And so on.

Rebirth has many names. Reincarnation (pronounced ree–in–car–NAE–tion) is the most popular. *Re* means again. *Incarnate* means to give flesh or body to something. Thus, reincarnation means to give another body to a soul or spirit.

Reincarnation is also called such difficult-to-pronounce names as metempsychosis (this is popular with scholars), palingenesis, transmigration, preexistence, and *samsara*, which means "the wheel of life," and is used by people in India.

The Beliefs of Famous People

Pythagoras

While belief in rebirth is as old as primitive man, the first historical person who believed in it was Pythagoras. High school students will recall him as the Greek mathematician who discovered the theorem we learn in geometry: "The square on the hypotenuse of a right triangle is equal to the sum of the squares of the other two sides."

In addition to being a founding father of mathematics, Pythagoras was a mystic who believed in the magic power of numbers.

He also believed he had lived other lives. In one of these he thought that he had been a Trojan who was killed when the Greeks burned the city of Troy in 1164 B.C.

Businesspeople

We are more likely to expect belief in reincarnation from astronomers who work with the vast sweep of space and stars than from hardheaded businessmen. Yet, Henry Ford, the classic example of the capitalist, was a strong believer.

Ford (1863–1947) manufactured the Ford automobile. He had the idea of using the conveyor belt and assembly line to produce a large number of cars cheaply. His novel methods ushered in the era of mass production.

Ford revealed his interest in reincarnation in a newspaper interview in 1938. He said that he had lost all interest in work when he was twenty-six. His mind overflowed with ideas he knew he would never have time to handle. It depressed him to think all the experience he was gaining would be lost when he died.

Then a friend gave him a small book on reincarnation. Ford was excited by what he read. His interest in life and work returned.

"Work is futile if we cannot use our experience in another life," Ford told his interviewer. "When I first heard of reincarnation, I knew then that I was no longer limited by time."

Ford went on to say that many people thought that genius is a gift or talent. "This is untrue," the inventor said positively. "Genius is the fruit of long experience in many lives.

"Of this I am sure, we are here for a purpose. We will go on. Mind and memory—they are eternal."

Soldiers

Ford believed that his inventions were made possible by experience he gained in other lives. In a similar manner a very famous soldier believed that his success in World War II was due to his battlefield experiences in other times.

This soldier was the colorful General George Patton (1885–1945). Patton loved war and fighting. In World War II, he commanded Allied troops in North Africa and Sicily. He led U.S. forces in battles against the Germans, from France all the way to Czechoslovakia. Although he was a wealthy man, he remained in the army because he loved military life. His recklessness and daring caused newspaper reporters to call him "Blood and Guts" Patton. His soldiers added ruefully, "Yeah, *our* blood and *his* guts!"

Patton strongly believed in reincarnation. He thought that he had once fought as a legion commander in Caesar's army. He was sure that he had been there when the Greeks built the great Trojan horse that led to the fall of Troy. He also—if you believe him—fought beside Richard the Lion-Hearted in the Third Crusade (A.D. 1189–1199) to free the Holy Land from the Saracens.

Patton was equally certain that he would go on fighting wars in future lives as he had in past ones. He made this clear in a poem he wrote. One line of the poem reads, "So forever in the future, shall I battle as of yore."

Writers

Many famous writers have believed in rebirth. Ovid, the Roman poet who lived from 43 B.C. to A.D. 17, wrote:

> *Then death, so call'd, is but old matter dress'd*
> *In some new figure, and a varied vest;*
> *Thus all things are but alter'd, nothing dies;*
> *And here and there the unbodied spirit flies . . .*
> *. . . The form only is changed, the wax is still the same*
> *So death, so called, can but the form deface,*
> *The mortal soul flies out in empty space;*
> *To seek her fortune in some other place.*

This translation of Ovid is by John Dryden, England's poet laureate from 1670 to 1688. Dryden, of course, is only echoing the thoughts of Ovid. But the poet showed his own belief in reincarnation in "An Ode to the Memory of Mrs. Killigrew." The lady had been a dear friend. Dryden wrote that earlier poets must have written about her in her other lives.

Henry David Thoreau is a famous name from nineteenth-century American literature. In a letter to Emerson in July 1843, Thoreau wrote: "And Hawthorne, too, I remember as one with whom I walked in old heroic times along the banks of the Scamander amid the ruins of chariots and heroes."

Hawthorne is Nathaniel Hawthorne, author of *The House of the Seven Gables* and other famous novels. The

Scamander is the river that flows past the ancient site of Troy.

Views that people hold when young often change as they age. Thoreau's belief in reincarnation did not. Ten years after he wrote that he and Hawthorne had been at Troy in 1164 B.C., he said in another letter to Harrison Blake: "As the stars looked down at me when I was a shepherd in Assyria, they look down at me now a New Englander."

These are but two examples of several references to Thoreau's belief in reincarnation that can be found in his collected letters.

"I Lived While Troy Was . . ."

A lot of famous people who believed in reincarnation have claimed to have been at Troy. Caracalla, the Roman emperor, believed himself to be the reincarnation of Achilles, the Greek hero killed at Troy.

In Homer's *Iliad* there is an account of a splendid funeral Achilles gave for his friend Patroklos. So when a friend of Caracalla's died, the emperor gave the dead man a funeral exactly like the one Homer described. Since Caracalla was half-crazy, enemies whispered that he killed his friend to have an excuse for the funeral.

Charles C. Emerson was the brother of the more famous Ralph Waldo Emerson. Once Charles wrote: "The reason why Homer's *Iliad* is to me like a dewy morning is because I too lived while Troy was. I sailed in the hollow ships of the Grecians to sack the city."

Asked why the rest of us cannot read our past lives as he could, Emerson replied, "People are drugged with the sleep bowl of the present. But when something strikes a hidden chord of memory in the soul, we remember our past lives."

Emerson was a brilliant young man who died in 1836 at the age of twenty-eight. Those who knew him thought that if he had lived Charles might have surpassed the fame of his brother.

Kings and Statesmen

Even kings have been believers. On his deathbed in 1786, Frederick the Great of Prussia said bitterly, "I am convinced that nothing is destroyed in nature. So I know for a certainty that the more noble part of me [that is, the soul] will not die. Though I may not be a king in my future life, so much the better. I shall nevertheless live an active life, and, on top of it, earn less ingratitude."

We can see from this that the great king was not happy with the way his people treated him.

Napoleon, emperor of France, said on several occasions, "I am Charlemagne!" He believed himself to be the reincarnation of the great Frankish king who lived from 742 to 814. Charlemagne established an empire that was later called the Holy Roman Empire. He became Emperor of the West in 800.

Winston Churchill, the leader of Great Britain in World War II, said he did not believe in reincarnation. However, he admitted that it was possible. He said that it was possible that he might be reborn a Chinese coolie in a later life. "And I shall certainly protest!" he said.

Churchill had an odd sense of humor at times. It is difficult to know if he was serious or just making a joke in this case.

But What Proof Do They Have?

These are but a few scattered examples of famous people who have believed that we have other lives. We cannot believe in rebirth ourselves just because a large number of famous people believed in it. Their beliefs might be enough to make us seriously consider the idea. But the famous can be as wrong about something as the rest of us.

We are right to ask these people what proof they have to offer us. We must have more than just their opinions. We cannot agree with Edgar Allan Poe who wrote in *Berenice:* "It is mere idleness to say that I had not lived before—that the soul has no previous existence. You deny it?—let us not argue the matter. Convinced myself, I seek not to convince."

The rest of us may not be so convinced. We need something other than General Patton's belief that he fought at Troy. Or that Thoreau believed he had been an Assyrian shepherd. Or that Henry Ford gained his knowledge in earlier lifetimes.

The Case of Hélène Smith

The famous case of Hélène Smith is a reason why we must be wary of accepting a claim just because a well-known person made it.

Thomas Flournoy was a famous professor of psychology at the University of Geneva in Switzerland. He heard of Hélène Smith (whose real name was Muller) and how she was making odd statements. Flournoy went to see her. She was a large, energetic Swiss woman. She told Flournoy that five hundred years ago he had been Prince Nayaka in a small Indian kingdom.

The professor checked history books. He found no reference to such a prince or kingdom. He consulted historians. None of these had heard of the place either. Then Flournoy chanced upon an obscure book. It mentioned a Prince Nayaka who built a giant fortress in a small kingdom called Nanara in India.

This startled Flournoy, for there was no evidence that Hélène could have seen the book. He studied her claims intently for some time, and then wrote a book in 1896 about her. It was called *From India to the Planet Mars*. It took an unsympathetic view of Miss Smith. While there was much he could not explain, he did not believe her claims.

The book revealed that Miss Smith claimed to recall

other lives she had lived. She had been a princess in India, a woman of the time of Christ, and Queen Marie Antoinette, who was beheaded in the French Revolution. But most startling of all was Hélène's claim that she could talk to the spirits of the recent dead. From these she could learn their new incarnations.

She told one mother that her son, dead for fifteen years, had been reincarnated on the planet Mars. Later she was able to describe the young man's life on the planet. Her description of the Martian world was not too different from Earth.

Then in 1896 Hélène topped her Martian tales by making a speech in what she said was the Martian language. The speech began with these words: *"Mitchma mitchmon minimi tchousainem--"*

The startling thing was that her words were not gibberish. Scholars said they seemed to be formed according to rules of grammar. This caused a lot of people to ignore Flournoy's skepticism, building Hélène a strong following.

She continued to tell about life on Mars until her death in 1930. As late as 1960 she was being quoted in occult books as evidence to support reincarnation.

Unfortunately for Hélène's occult reputation, an unmanned spacecraft landed on Mars in 1975. Its television cameras saw none of the cities and people she described. All was desolation. A mechanical arm dug into the red soil, placing the dirt in a container for analysis. The experiment failed to find even so much as a germ to prove that any kind of life had ever lived on the planet.

Theosophical Beliefs

It has been claimed, without any real evidence, that Hélène was inspired to become an occultist after reading about Madame Helena Petrovna Blavatsky. In 1875 Madame Blavatsky, in association with Colonel Olcott, formed the Theosophical Society. Theosophy, as Madame Blavatsky explained in a series of books, is a Wisdom Religion. Madame said she learned of it through higher intelligences, living on a different plane, who chose her to be their mouthpiece. It is a complicated philosophy, containing elements suggestive of Hinduism, Buddhism, and Madame's own ideas. We are not concerned with it here, except as it deals with her ideas of reincarnation.

She taught that man is composed of several principles. These are divided into a lower (mortal) and a higher (immortal) nature. When a person dies, the higher nature ascends to heaven, where its happiness depends upon the degree of the person's goodness on earth. The soul (higher nature) does not stay permanently in heaven. After its goodness has been used up, the soul returns to earth for a new rebirth.

Here it is joined again with its lower nature. This cycle of death and rebirth continues until the higher nature purges itself of all the lower-nature corruption.

This is, despite differences in the constitution of the higher and lower natures, much like Hinduism. In Hinduism it is one's *karma*—product of good and bad deeds—that require the soul to be reborn again and again to purge itself of earthly sins.

When we deal with religious, philosophic, or personal claims of reincarnation, we often have to depend upon faith and our belief in those who bring us the messages. All too often, these turn out, like Hélène Smith, to be wrong.

Fortunately, we do not have to depend solely upon the unproven word and claims of people—people who may be sincere but who are still wrong.

There are a number of things that might point toward the possibility of reincarnation. One of these is the curious feeling people often get when it seems to them that they have done or seen something before. This is called *déjà vu,* a French term that means "already seen."

● 2 ●

Shadowy Memories

Why is it that some scenes awaken thoughts that belong, as it were, to dreams of early and shadowy recollections? . . . How often do we find ourselves in society which we have never before met. Yet we feel impressed with a mysterious and ill-defined feeling that neither the scene nor the speakers nor the subject are entirely new.

This question was asked by Sir Walter Scott in his novel *Guy Mannering*. A student of reincarnation can easily answer Sir Walter's question. This is déjà vu, the feeling that we have done something before although we cannot recall having done so.

Déjà vu—already seen—is one of the proofs that believers give us to support their claims that reincarnation really happens. Many examples of déjà vu can be found in books on rebirth.

A typical account of déjà vu is the story of a young man from the South who visited friends in New England. These friends took him to visit some people who lived in a very old house that dated back to colonial times.

When the young man entered the house he had a strange uneasy feeling that he had been there. Yet he had never been in New England before. Nor could he recall ever being in a house like this one anywhere.

His uneasiness did not go away. It increased. Suddenly he blurted out to his host, "Is there a secret room in this house?"

The host looked oddly at him. "Why do you ask?" he said.

The young man was embarrassed. "I don't know," he replied. "The question just slipped out." He apologized for his rudeness.

"This is very odd," the host said. "There is no secret room in this house. However—there was one once!"

He went on to tell a story. When his family bought the house in 1907, there had been a secret room behind the stairwell on the second floor. The story was that the room had been built around the time of the Revolutionary War. The family who lived in the house then had a member who was mentally unbalanced. The family tried to keep this a secret by imprisoning the lunatic in the secret room.

Other owners left the room until the host's father removed it to enlarge a bedroom in 1912. The host had forgotten about the room, in which he had played as a child, until his guest's question recalled it to his mind.

What caused the young man to suddenly blurt out his question? He never knew. There was nothing in the conversation to make him ask. It just popped into his mind, along with the uneasy feeling that he had been in this house before.

He continued to think about this weird experience. He made inquiries among members of his family after he returned home. The family originally lived in New England, moving to the South after the Civil War. They came from the section where the old house was located.

Now the question in the young man's mind was: "Is there some connection through reincarnation between me and this house?

"Am I the one who built that secret room to hide someone the family feared for neighbors to see?" he asks. "Or—and this frightens me most of all—could I have been the murderous lunatic the room was built *for!*"

A Glimpse of the Past

Memories of other lives do not necessarily have to be pleasant ones. Actually, déjà vu is not a full memory of an experience or a place we may have visited in the past. The sight or experience of today strikes a bell deep in our subconscious minds, giving us a brief glimpse of the past. This stirs ancient memories, but not enough to give us full recognition of the person, place, or event. All we receive is an uneasy, puzzling feeling that there is something we *should* remember.

Psychic investigators have estimated that at least half the people of the United States have felt déjà vu at one time or another. This does not mean that so many have been caused by reincarnation. Some such feelings may be inspired by something read, heard, or imagined, and then forgotten.

In true déjà vu there is apparently no connection with the recollection and anything read or heard about. It is such cases as these that make one wonder.

One such is General Patton's visit to some Roman ruins in France. A local man offered to guide the general. Although he had never been there before, Patton said, "That is not necessary. I *know* this place."

As they went through the ruins, Patton kept pointing out such things as the parade ground, the stone barracks where the soldiers slept, and the temple where they prayed to Mars, their god of war. The French guide was amazed, but Patton was not surprised at all. He firmly believed that he had been there in Roman times.

In the case of Joan Grant, the British writer, déjà vu led to a surprising ending. In 1935 Ms. Grant visited Luxor, the site of the ancient capital of Egypt. The Egyptian guide took her across the Nile River to visit the ruins of the famous temple of Hatshepsut (HAT-cheap-suit), a curious queen of old Egypt who became the only woman to rule the ancient kingdom.

Most people are awed when they see the temple rising up against the towering cliff behind it. Ms. Grant's feeling was surprise that an avenue of trees that led down to the Nile was now missing.

At the time she had no idea why she knew that there had once been a tree-lined road there. Later she said she found out why the sight of the temple caused this sense of déjà vu. "I had spent the best part of two thousand years in the Nile Valley," she wrote in *Many Lifetimes,* a book written in 1967 with her present husband, Denys Kelsey.

This déjà vu was a beginning. Then eighteen months later the sight of a stone scarab in the home of a friend loosened her memory of other lives.

These ancient memories flooded through her mind. She had been Sekeeta, daughter of a pharaoh three thousand years ago. These recollections were written down and became the book, *The Winged Pharoah.* Ms. Grant called her book a posthumous autobiography. She tells us that it is true, recalled through "far memory." Not everyone agrees with this. Some libraries I have checked have the book filed under fiction. You may also find it in others filed in the occult and parapsychology sections.

Joan Grant is one of those unusual people who claim to have total recall of their past lives. She seems to remember the smallest details. In addition to *Winged Pharaoh,* she has written about another life she lived in Egypt, and about her lives in Greece and as an American Indian.

Shocking Recollections

Most cases of déjà vu leave us with a sense of puzzlement. But occasionally we feel or see cases of unnerving shocks. I have seen this happen one time, and it happened to me on two occasions.

Witness to a Recollection

The case I saw was in Egypt. It was during one of my three trips to Luxor, the ancient city of Thebes. I had already seen the Valley of the Kings, the tomb of Tutankhamen, and the Colossi of Memnon. This time I wanted to see the tombs of the nobles. These are not as richly decorated as the tombs of the kings. Tourists do not usually go to these unless they are really interested in ancient Egypt. This is unfortunate, for they are very interesting and well worth a trip.

At the travel office I asked about arranging a special tour to the tombs. I was told that they were taking two other parties to the same place. I could join them. One was a man and his wife. They were from California. The other was a woman about forty-five years old. She said she was from Los Angeles. She was a quiet woman who only spoke when someone asked her a question.

We visited two of the nobles' tombs and then went to what the guide called the Tomb of Nakht. As we got to the steps leading a few feet down into the tomb, the woman began to tremble violently. Then she started to cry. She sank down on the stone steps as if her legs had grown too weak to support her.

Naturally we all rushed to her aid. Through the sobs that shook her body she kept saying, "I'm sorry! I'm sorry! I don't know what's come over me!"

The guide was greatly alarmed. He looked at me appealingly. I suggested that we pass up this tomb. It is not considered an important one anyway. We helped her back to the car. Her fear—or whatever it was—gradually left her as we got farther away from the Tomb of Nakht.

You sometimes find people who are psychic who like to put on displays and shows to attract attention. I first suspected this here. The number of fakers in the psychic field is enormous. I do not think that this was true in this case. The woman was genuinely embarrassed by her experience. When we got back to the Winter Palace Hotel in Luxor, she avoided the rest of us at dinner that evening. Then she cut short her tour by one day, leaving by plane for Cairo the next morning. Fakers do not withdraw like this. They want to enjoy the effect they have upon others.

I was sorry she left. I would have liked to have talked to her about her exact feeling and thoughts at the moment of her breakdown on the steps of Nakht. I believe it was caused by a very strong sense of déjà vu.

Later I went back to the tomb. I was curious to see if I could find anything that might have caused her odd behavior. I found nothing.

The tomb is small and quite ordinary. Nakht was Scribe of the Granaries—he kept the records of grain stored between harvests. One wall was covered with picture writing from *The Book of the Dead*. This is common in many tombs. It gives instructions for the dead person on how to get to the underworld to have his spirit judged.

Other scenes showed everyday life in Nakht's family. There was even a cat eating under his table. The only thing of importance that I could see was the painting of three teenage dancing girls. This is a well-known picture. It is often reproduced on postcards, plates, and other tourist souvenirs.

I could not connect that stocky, graying woman with those delightful young girls—or with anything else in the tomb. Of course, if this really was a genuine déjà vu, three thousand years can certainly make a big difference!

I never saw the lady again. Anything I can say other than what I actually saw would be nothing but guesses. And guesswork is the greatest mistake a serious investigator can make.

My Own Recollections

In the course of writing more than eighty published books, I have traveled to many far places of the world. Four or five times I have experienced a sense of déjà vu in some of these odd scenes.

Stone Windows in the Sky

One I remember particularly, for it was exceptionally strong, was in Aksum, Ethiopia, in 1972. According to Ethiopian legend, the Queen of Sheba lived in Aksum about 970 B.C. She heard of Solomon's wisdom and went to Jerusalem to meet him. A son was born to Solomon and Sheba. This boy later became Menelik I, the first emperor of Ethiopia.

Today only some crumbling mud brick walls and a few strange stone shafts remain as reminders that Aksum was once a powerful capital of a great empire.

The shafts are slender needles of stone. A locked door is carved at the bottom. Above the door the shafts are carved with window frames that reach all the way to the top, which is crowned with a crescent moon. Some of the shafts are 100 feet high. No one knows what they mean, for nothing like them has been found anywhere else in the world.

Looking at these strange shafts, I was suddenly struck by a feeling I had seen them before. Actually, I had never seen even a picture of them. This made the feeling the more curious.

After the heavy Ethiopian rains rushing water uncovers relics of the lost city. Boys pick these up and sell them to visitors. One brought me an odd and badly corroded three inch bronze image of a king on a throne. He had a skull-like head with bulging eyes and a thick slash for a mouth. He is far from pretty, but he is interesting. He sits today on the edge of my bookcase where I can look up from my writing and see him.

I remembered how Joan Grant's far memories were jogged into life by staring at an Egyptian scarab. I have stared at that stubborn little king many times in a similar manner in the seven years I have owned him.

He does absolutely nothing for me.

Yet, I cannot shake the déjà vu feeling that I have

seen those shafts of Aksum sometime, somewhere. If we believe the reincarnation claims of Patton and others, then souls jump around in different nationalities. Was I once an Ethiopian warrior? Or a sailor captured from a Roman warship defeated by the Aksumites in 350 B.C.? Maybe I was the Greek trader who visited Aksum in A.D. 100 and then wrote an account of it. Or one of the shipwrecked boys who brought Christianity to Ethiopia in A.D. 325? Or maybe a soldier in the British army that invaded the country in 1867 to punish the king for mistreating a British consul?

My little bronze king does not tell me. And none of these possibilities strike the slightest familiar note in my mind. Yet, I cannot shake the strange belief that once upon a time I saw those unusual shafts.

Three Red Suns

The strongest feeling of déjà vu—and the most shocking—that I ever felt was in Alaska in 1947. All my life I have hated and dreaded extreme cold weather. I was almost frantic when the U.S. Air Force—for no good reason that I could see—sent me up to this natural icebox.

It was not as bad as I thought it would be, but I never ceased to be uneasy when the temperature dropped below minus 35 degrees F (minus 1.6° C). Then one day about noon I was startled by a cry from a friend outside the building. He wanted me to come and see a "sun dog."

It was close to 50 below zero at that time. I did not want to stick my head out in that cold to see any kind of dog. But he kept yelling and I finally went.

Never before or since have I been so surprised.

I saw a world that looked like it was made of glass. And hanging just above the crystal trees were three suns in the sky. The one in the center was the largest and brightest. The ones on each side of it were smaller and deeper in color. They were all dim enough that you could look at them with the naked eye.

I felt as if I had taken a science fiction novel off the shelf and walked right into the pages. Later I learned that this sight is nothing particularly unusual, although one as clear as this did not happen often. Technically I think it is called a *parhelion* effect.

Heat from fires on the military base and from the city of Fairbanks, hitting the arctic air, created fog in the sky. This fog consisted of tiny ice crystals suspended in the air. Some had settled on the trees, coating them with ice that made the trees look like they had turned to glass.

The sun does not rise very high in the sky in these arctic winters. When conditions are just right, the ice crystals may act like prisms to project two mock suns, one on each side of the real sun. Often the mock suns are only blurs of light. But occasionally they are projected as round balls, slightly smaller than the real sun. Alaskans call these "sun dogs." One of Jack London's arctic tales was called *The Sun Dog Trail*.

While they are fairly common, I had never heard of them. So it was a genuine shock to see three orange-red suns hanging low over a crystal world.

The oddest thing about this experience was that as soon as I got over my first surprise I felt a strong sense of déjà vu. It was not the usual mild puzzlement. This was very strong, accompanied by a return of the uneasiness I often felt in extremely cold weather. I felt very strongly that I had seen this strange three-sun world before.

Different Ideas

I spoke of this experience to friends after I returned to the South in 1948. They thought I should speak to a psychic about it. I did—in fact I have talked to seven over the years. Every single one gave me a different explanation.

They all agreed that it was true déjà vu recollection of a previous incarnation. One said it was a memory of my murder while driving a dogsled mail team in the Klondike gold rush of 1898. The last thing I saw as I lay dying in the snow was a sun dog in the sky.

Another claimed I was recalling a time when I was an Eskimo in northern Canada. The most fanciful explanation was that my sun dog déjà vu was a shadow memory of a long ago time when I died fighting a saber-toothed tiger in the last Ice Age.

Do I believe any of these explanations?

No, I do not. If more than one had told the same story I might have believed. I do not mean by this that all were fakers. Many so-called psychics are sincere, but have deluded themselves.

Other Explanations

We must also keep in mind that déjà vu has never been proven to be connected with reincarnation. Some psychics say that it is not. These doubters say that it may be caused by psychometry. Psychometry (sie-CAHM-uh-tree) teaches that all things have memory records locked within them. A person with the right psychic mind possibly could tune in on these memories. Déjà vu may be a brief glimpse of these locked memories. Or so some people say.

This idea is hotly denied by believers in reincarnation, but it does raise a doubt. We are within our scientific rights to demand more proof than déjà vu before we accept reincarnation.

There are other ways to investigate the idea of rebirth. One of these is to use hypnotism to send a person's mind back to his or her other lives.

• 3 •

The Girl from Old Ireland

In 1954 the *Denver Post* newspaper published a story that a young woman in Pueblo, Colorado, could remember another life she had in Ireland.

The complete story was published as a book in 1956. It was called *The Search for Bridey Murphy* and was written by Morey Bernstein, a young Colorado businessman.

The book told how Bernstein had hypnotized a young woman. Through a standard hypnotic technique known as "age regression," Bernstein caused the woman to remember this past life.

The woman was called Ruth Mills Simmons in the book. It was later revealed that her real name was Virginia Burns Tighe. She was born April 27, 1923, in Madison, Wisconsin. The young girl she had once been was named Bridey Murphy, who was born in Cork, Ireland, in 1798.

The book created a sensation. It was chosen by a national book club. Sections from it were serialized in newspapers across the country. A national magazine ran a condensation of it. Everyone was talking about Bridey Murphy that spring of 1956.

It was nothing new for someone to claim that he or she remembered a past life. People have been doing that since the days of ancient Greece without arousing the public interest that Bridey Murphy did.

The big difference between Bridey Murphy and the other claims of past lives was that Bridey Murphy seemed real. Most other cases of reincarnation were merely claims put out by various people. There is no proof that any person claiming to have lived before actually did live another life. We have only that person's word for it.

The Bridey Murphy case seemed to offer more than just one person's claim. In this case, the person involved made no claim at all. A third person, Morey Bernstein, was supplying the evidence that Mrs. Simmons had once been an Irish girl named Bridey Murphy.

We were told that when Mrs. Simmons awoke from her hypnotic trip back into time, she could remember nothing of what she said. She had to listen to tape recordings made during the sessions. She was astonished herself at what Bernstein dredged from her subconscious mind. This gave an air of sincerity to the case that impressed the public, creating wide interest in Bridey.

How It All Began

Bernstein became interested in hypnotism ten years before he met Mrs. Simmons. During this time he heard about the work of Dr. J. B. Rhine of Duke University. For some years Dr. Rhine had been making scientific experiments in parapsychology. These experiments had created widespread interest.

The most publicized of the Rhine tests dealt with telepathy—mind reading at a distance. In these experiments Dr. Rhine used special cards. A man in one room selected a card. Another person in an adjoining room would try to identify the card through mental communication alone.

After reading about these tests in Dr. Rhine's book, *Reach of the Mind,* Bernstein wrote to ask if hypnotism had ever been used in tests for telepathy. Dr. Rhine replied that he had never used hypnotized subjects and he did not know of anyone who had.

Bernstein then decided to try his own tests, using two men he hypnotized. He hoped that hypnotism would sharpen their minds and increase the chances of making telepathy work.

The results of the tests were encouraging, but were not good enough. They were a little better than just plain guessing, but not so much better that they would convince doubters.

By this time Bernstein had become interested in rebirth. However, it did not occur to him to use hypnotism to test a person for other lives until he read a book by Sir Alexander Cannon, a British psychiatrist. Bernstein knew that hypnotists had used hypnotism to get subjects to recall forgotten incidents of their early childhood. He had often done this himself.

But Cannon had done more, Bernstein was startled to read. As Bernstein put it later, "Instead of stopping when the subject's memory reached infancy or birth, the *doctor kept right on going*. He probed still farther back, investigating the mystery of memories before birth."

This excited Bernstein. He gave up his experiments with telepathy and turned to age regression (sending the hypnotized mind back to earlier times and lives).

No one knows exactly how this is done. It seems to be done by unlocking the subconscious mind.

All of us have two minds. One is the conscious mind. This is the mind—thought processes—that directs our conscious activity.

But there are many actions that we do not deliberately make. These are done unconsciously, without our mind giving a direct order. We do not have to tell our heart to beat or our lungs to breathe. When we are asleep our conscious mind is turned off. It rests and renews itself. But our bodily work goes on. Decisions are made outside our normal thought processes. If a position gets uncomfortable during sleep, we roll over without receiving a direct command from our conscious mind.

We also dream and some of these dreams are far removed from reality. They are often something we would never consciously conjure up.

Holder of Old Secrets

This activity comes from the subconscious mind—the mind below the normal mind. It apparently never sleeps. It also appears to be less forgetful than the conscious mind, holding on to old secrets long after the normal mind has forgotten them. So the idea of age regression (to send back to earlier ages) is to lock out the conscious mind by hypnotic trance and to question the subconscious.

Age regression has been used successfully to get people to recall forgotten incidents of their past life. If reincarnation is real and if it is possible for memories of these other lives to remain with us, then these memories would be stored in our subconscious minds.

These were the memories that Bernstein—following the lead he got from Sir Alexander Cannon's book—wanted to unlock. After considering several people, he decided to use the woman he called Mrs. Simmons in his book, *The Search for Bridey Murphy*. He had hypnotized Mrs. Simmons several times before. She was an easy subject, slipping without effort into the hypnotic trance.

The experiment began in a partially darkened room. Bernstein held a candle flame close to the woman's eyes. He focused her attention upon the flame. Then in a soothing voice he began to talk to her about the flame and sleep. This was followed by suggestions that she was growing sleepy.

After Mrs. Simmons went into hypnotic sleep, the

hypnotist kept suggesting that she was going into a deeper and still deeper sleep. He suggested that she was seven years old and asked a number of questions about her life at that age.

He then took her back to still earlier ages, finally telling her to remember things she saw when she was one year old. Up to this point Bernstein was merely repeating what he had done before. Now came the crucial, exciting point. He would try to take her subconscious memories back beyond her last birth to another life in another time.

She had stopped talking. Bernstein's soft, whispering voice continued. He told her she was going back, back, back. "You will find yourself in some other scene, in some other place, in some other time."

Bernstein kept talking. Finally he said, "Tell me what scenes come to your mind. What do you see?"

When she finally spoke, Mrs. Simmons said that she had scratched paint from her newly painted bed. She did it for spite. More questions brought out that she was recalling a girlhood in Cork, Ireland, in the year 1806. She said her name was Bridey Murphy.

Six Sessions with "Bridey Murphy"

Bernstein continued to question Bridey Murphy through six sessions stretching through 1952 and 1953. He asked hundreds of detailed questions. All questions and answers were recorded on tape for closer study.

Bernstein played the tapes for friends and some professional people. The *Denver Post* ran three articles about Bridey Murphy in 1954. But it was not until Bernstein's book appeared in January 1956 that most people heard about her.

The book became an immediate best seller. Those who believed in reincarnation hailed it as proof of their beliefs. However, many psychiatrists, historians, and religious figures disagreed violently with the book.

Those who disagreed did not for the most part call it a fraud. This was because of the way the book was written. Bernstein explained hypnotism and what he was trying to do with it. He told of other work by different hypnotists in age regression. Bernstein followed this with an explanation of how Mrs. Simmons was hypnotized, the questions he asked her, and the answers she gave. It is hard to read the book without being impressed by Bernstein's sincerity. He believed in what he was doing and honestly tried to conduct a fair test.

At the same time, no one questioned Mrs. Simmons sincerity either. She was hypnotized and did not know what she said as Bridey Murphy until she was awakened and listened to the tapes made of her Irish talk.

Basis for Disagreement

Then why did so many professional people disagree? Why did major newspapers and magazines—*Time,* for example—try to prove that there had been no age regression at all?

Some, of course, just did not believe in reincarnation. Therefore, anything that tends to prove it is wrong. Others did not agree that hypnotism gave truthful answers. Still others objected upon religious grounds. Reincarnation is a basic belief in two of the world's great religions, Hinduism and Buddhism. Although we can find traces of a belief in reincarnation in both Judaism and Christianity, these two religions generally deny that this kind of rebirth is possible.

Both *Life* magazine and the *Chicago American* newspaper tried to prove that there could have been no Bridey Murphy. The *American* traced back Mrs. Simmons's life. They found that when she was a small child she lived near a woman named Birdie Murphy Corkell. The reporters also found other people with names similar to those Bridey Murphy spoke of. From this, the newspaper claimed that all Mrs. Simmons said under hypnosis were just forgotten snatches of memory from her childhood in this life.

But what about the things she said about Ireland? Bridey Murphy named names, told of places, and described conditions in 1806.

First, investigators in Ireland could find no record of a Bridey Murphy being born. It seems that births were not recorded until 1864. She said her father was a lawyer. No record could be found of a lawyer named Murphy in Cork. Historians said people did not use metal beds in Ireland in 1806. Therefore,

Bridey could not have scraped the paint off one. They claimed that they could find no record of any of the people she named. And so on through a long list of objections.

The *Denver Post*, which was the first newspaper to print a story about Bridey Murphy, decided that investigators sent to Ireland by the other papers and magazines had not dug deep enough. One only spent three days checking out Bridey's story. The *Post* then sent William J. Barker, the writer of their first Bridey Murphy stories, to Cork. His job was to find anything that would help prove Bridey's story.

He found things that disproved some of the objections to Bridey's story. There *were* metal bedsteads in Ireland at this time. She said she had bought things in stores owned by men named Farr and Carrigan. Barker found that both men had grocery stores in Belfast, Ireland, where Bridey lived after her marriage in 1815.

Barker made one very strong point. Bridey said she lived as a child in a place she called "the meadows." Historians claimed there was no such place in Cork. Barker found a map made in Ireland in 1801. On it is a suburb set away from town. This area is marked Mardike Meadows. Seven buildings, widely separated from each other, are shown on the Meadows.

This does not prove that one of the houses was the home of Bridey Murphy. It does show that one could have been and could have been called "the meadows."

Barker found other things to support Bridey Murphy. He put them all in a story entitled, "The Truth About Bridey Murphy." The story appeared in the March 11, 1956, issue of the *Denver Post*.

At this point we have one side saying no and one saying yes. Each side presented evidence based upon Bridey's own words. Which side is right?

A Professor Investigates

In 1962 C. J. Ducasse of Brown University, Rhode Island, investigated the claims of both sides. Here is what Ducasse said about those who disagreed:

"Neither the articles in magazines and newspapers . . . nor the comments of authors of the so-called 'Scientific Reports' and other psychiatrists . . . have succeeded in disproving, or even in establishing a case against, the possibility that many of the statements of the Bridey personality are genuine memories of an earlier life . . . over a century ago in Ireland."

This would appear that Ducasse believed Mrs. Simmons to be the reincarnation of Bridey Murphy. However, the professor disagreed with this in his next paragraph. He said that the things Barker found during his visit to Ireland "do not prove that Virginia [Mrs. Simmons' real first name] is a reincarnation of Bridey, nor do they establish a particularly strong case for it."

Now what do we have? This careful investigator disagrees with both sides. Then what does he agree with?

He agreed on the sincerity of Bridey's statements and on Barker's investigation in Ireland. He did not disagree with the fact that Bridey seemed to have recalled correct information about Ireland.

The way Ducasse put it in professorial language is: "They do, on the other hand, constitute fairly strong evidence that, in the hypnotic trances, *paranormal* knowledge of one or another of several possible kinds concerning these recondite facts of nineteeth-century Ireland, become manifest."

What does this mean?

It appears to mean that the professor does not believe in reincarnation, but does believe that something other than normal was working through Mrs. Simmons while she was hypnotized.

What is this something? Ducasse only called it "*paranormal* knowledge of several possible kinds." Paranormal means above normal. He did not say what the "several possible kinds" are.

Telepathy has been suggested as one of these. She subconsciously read the minds of other people to pick up facts that she confused in her own mind. Another suggestion was "ancestral memories." Ancestral memories are different from "racial memories," which are inherited traits of a race or species. These are the things we do by instinct. Ancestral memories, if there is such a thing, would be memories that occurred in the life or lives of our immediate ancestors and were carried down like our inherited traits in the human seed.

One of the objections raised to déjà vu as a "proof"

of reincarnation is that these curious feelings are really caused by ancestral memories, rather than something that occurred to us in another life.

Another possibility of the "several possible kinds" of things Professor Ducasse spoke of is spirits. Spiritualists have suggested that the spirit of a dead woman was talking through Bridey, using her as a medium while she was in her hypnotic trance.

There are other possibilities, but none of these have been proven. Suggestions have been raised that in such cases the hypnotist may have "led" the subject through suggestions. This was not raised in any of the major investigations of Bridey Murphy, either by Professor Ducasse, the *Chicago American,* or *Life* magazine. There was no suggestion of fraud. Bernstein's sincerity was not questioned. This was because the tapes of his sessions with Mrs. Simmons were available for serious investigators to listen to. Any leading on his part would be readily detectable.

We must put down Bridey Murphy as an interesting attempt to prove reincarnation.

It did not do so.

But neither did it prove that reincarnation is not true.

So the search for proof goes on.

• 4 •

The Soul and Reincarnation

Often when one asks a believer how people come back in a new form, the answer is, "They are born in the usual way."

This is not an answer we can accept. Before we can believe in reincarnation we must be given a logical way it can happen.

There are hundreds of questions that no one can answer yet. One is how the old soul gets back in a new body. All things grow from seeds, except elemental forms that split off from themselves. Animal life—including human—grows from eggs in the mother's body. We know how the egg is formed, fertilized, grows, and then is born to create a new life.

At what point, how, and why did the ancient soul get into this new egg? The egg and later the body are just the shell that carries the real life, which is soul.

Do We Have a Choice?

Now we come to another important question. Does the old soul have a choice as to which body it will reenter for its next life? Must it remain in the same family? Can it cross races and continents? How long does it wait? Is it forced to be reborn? At what point between death and rebirth does the memory fade? Does the soul lose its memory of the old life immediately after death? Or does it carry its memories to the point of rebirth? What happens to blur this past memory in most of us? Are we intended to forget? Are those who remember accidents who failed the forgetful stage?

There are different opinions on all these questions. As to whether we have a choice in our rebirth, Dr. Helen Womback, Ph.D., wrote an article in the January-February 1977 issue of *Psychic* magazine. It told of her work in age regression under hypnosis.

Dr. Womback studied 173 people. Only 5 percent said they had no choice in being reborn. One subject, a twin, said it was her sister who talked her into being reborn. She was afraid, and she recalls her twin saying, "OK, I'll go first."

Dr. Womback's subjects disagreed on when they entered the living body. Fifteen percent said it was after the baby was born. Thirty-three percent said their souls entered just before the baby was born. Others reported different times.

Can we believe these stories? We can give them the same recognition that we choose to give Bridey Murphy or any other age-regression experiment. All we can do is place our faith in the hypnotist.

The Mind of a Hypnotized Person

We do not know what goes on in the mind of a hypnotized person. Such people take suggestions readily. Doubters claim that the subjects take the hypnotist's questions for suggestions, telling him what he wants to hear. Another claim is that the so-called age-regression accounts are from the same source that produces dreams. In all fairness, we cannot really say that they are truly memories.

The human mind is still a great mystery. We do not know how it works or even what intelligence really is. Neither do we fully understand dreams. Dreams have been called everything from visions of the future to mental trouble.

While no one knows what really causes dreams, the condition of one's body has some effect. For example, a heavy meal that does not digest well may cause a nightmare. But the food does not determine *what* we dream. If it did, we could repeat the dream by giving ourselves another case of indigestion with the same food.

Some peculiar action of the brain determines the

often strange adventures we have in dreams. No one knows exactly what a hypnotic trance is, but it has been compared to sleep by some hypnotists. Therefore, are the things these hypnotic subjects tell about their other lives only dreams sparked by the questions asked of them? Or are they really memories of past lives?

If reincarnation is possible, then something must pass from the old body to the new one. This something must carry personality, experience, and memory. Otherwise, it is not the same person who is born again.

This something that passes from the old to the new body is the human soul. In religion, the soul is the spiritual force that is God-given. It is what makes a body live.

Beyond this general definition, no one can say what the soul is, what it looks like, how it connects to the body, or how it leaves when the body dies. Many people have given their ideas of the soul, but none has invented a test to demonstrate what it is.

How do we know it is there? Because it is the difference between a live body and a dead one. It is life itself. Just what this life form—soul—looks like is anybody's guess. In popular ghost stories the spirit looks just like the dead person. The ghost even wears the same clothing! This hardly makes sense, unless we admit that clothing has a spirit too.

The Spirit of Samuel

In the Holy Bible there is an account of a spirit. In Samuel I we read that King Saul of Israel is facing a battle with the Philistines. He is afraid and wants to know how the battle will turn out. So he forces a witch, the woman of Endore, to call up the ghost of the prophet Samuel to read the future.

As Samuel appears, Saul fearfully asks the witch, "What form is he of?"

The witch replies, "An old man comes up. He is covered with a mantle."

Since the prophet is covered by a mantle, Saul could not have seen its face. However, we are told that he recognized the spirit as Samuel. From this we can deduce that the ghostly form was pretty much as it had been in life.

The idea that the spirit is a shadowy image of the living is as old as humankind. Those who study the customs, legends, and folklore of primitive people tell us that this idea probably originated in dreams.

The caveman knew that he had bedded down in his cave at night. In the morning he awoke and was still there. *But* in the night he had left the cave to live strange adventures. Then by morning he was back in the cave, after fighting mammoths, falling off mountains, or whatever turn his dream took.

One of the differences between humankind and lower animals is the human hunger to know "why?" We seek a reason for all things. It was clear to the thinking caveman that he had never left his cave. Yet he remembered having strange adventures in far places. In the course of time, as his mind developed, he asked how he could have been in two places at once.

An answer, of course, was that there were really two of him. Inside his body was a separate him—a him that was invisible, but that could leave the body at night to go adventuring.

This person or thing was not a separate being. It was himself, for did he not remember everything that happened to it during these nightly adventures?

Another Step Forward

It is easy to use such an experience to make a giant step forward. The living body is like the log the caveman used to help him float across a stream. It is just something to carry the real person, the invisible life within him that can leave the body behind to go adventuring.

The idea of the human soul developed from this primitive beginning. Once the idea of the soul was accepted, the next step was to wonder what happened to the invisible being within when the body died and decayed.

At this point the developing mind of the caveman—or what became cavemen—had now grown enough in mind to understand the idea of God and religion.

Once we accept the idea of a life force within us that is separate from our living body, the next step is to wonder if this other self can return to a new body.

Reincarnation gives a possible answer. If a life force can enter a body in the first place, is there any reason that it cannot enter another new one later?

While legends indicate that early man believed in rebirth, the first civilized people to teach reincarnation were the Hindus of India. This information comes from Apollonius of Tyana. Apollonius is a mystic figure who lived about the time of Christ. What we know of him comes from a biography by Philostratus, who based his account upon notes taken by Damis, the sage's companion. Traveling in India, Apollonius met Iarchas, an Indian teacher in Kashmir.

Appollonius asked Iarchas, "What view do you take of the soul?"

Iarchas replied, "The same that Pythagoras taught you." He went on to say that Pythagoras got his ideas of reincarnation from the Egyptians, which Apollonius knew. Then the Indian added, "This knowledge we imparted to the Egyptians."

The Hindu people originated in the high steppes of central Asia. For some unknown reason they left their homeland about 3,000 B.C. They spread over different parts of Europe. One group came to India to become the Hindus. This group brought with them from their original home the religious beliefs—if we can believe Iarchas—that formed our present ideas of the human soul and its ability to be born again.

Apollonius noticed a sullen young man watching

them. He asked Iarchas about him. The Indian replied, "This young man was once Palamedes of Troy."

He went on to tell how Palamedes was killed by Odysseus at Troy. Homer failed to mention Palamedes' bravery in the *Iliad*. The memory of his death by a Greek's hand and the failure of the Greek poet to give him his due carried over into the young man's Indian incarnation. It made him hate all things Greek.

Apollonius asked for some proof that the young Indian had really been reincarnated. Iarchas said the proof was in the fact that the young Indian could read and write Greek—although no one had ever taught him. Nor was there any opportunity for him to have taught himself. That meant, Iarchas insisted, that the boy recalled the language from some previous incarnation.

Socrates, the great Classical Age teacher, who lived in Athens from about 470 B.C. to 399 B.C., used exactly the same argument four hundred years before Apollonius to prove that a young slave had lived before.

Socrates was an unusual type of teacher. While he left no writing of his own, his thoughts and ideas were preserved by his student Plato. Socrates had a brilliant way of getting his students to learn. He would ask their opinions and then question them sharply about their views. Gradually, through their own answers, they came to see their mistakes in reasoning. The mistakes did not have to be pointed out to them.

Plato listened and recorded these *Dialogues,* as they are called. They have had tremendous impact upon Western thought.

The argument Socrates used that is so close to that of Iarchas talking to Apollonius is in the Socratic Dialogue called *Memo.* Socrates approaches his friend Memo.

"I have heard the most wonderful thing," Socrates said.

Memo asked what it was. Socrates replied, "They say the soul of man is immortal. At one time it has an end, which is dying. At another time it is born again, but it is never destroyed."

Socrates went on to say that since the soul is immortal, it has lived many times. It has seen all things both in the present world, the times of the past, and in the spirit world.

"Since the soul knows all things," Socrates said, "one should be able to recollect these things if one works hard at it and does not faint. All learning is but the recollection of past experiences."

Memo, like Apollonius before him, wanted proof. Socrates then asked Memo to call one of his slaves. He asked the young man many questions about mathematics. The slave gave them the correct answers in every case.

Socrates then asked Memo: "You told me that this slave was born and reared in your house. Did you or anyone ever teach him mathematics?"

"I am certain he was never taught," Memo replied.

"If he did not learn in this life, then he must have learned in another life?"

"It would seem so," Memo replied.

"Then be of good cheer, and try to recollect what you do not remember."

Later, Socrates was accused of spoiling the minds of youth. He was sentenced to drink hemlock, a poison. He spent his final hours talking with his students about the human soul.

Socrates said that he recalled an "ancient doctrine" that claimed that people were born again after death. Then he said, "If it is true that the living come from the dead, then our souls must exist in another world. For if not, how could they be born again?"

Later Socrates said, "I am confident that there truly is such a thing as living again, and that the living spring from the dead."

Many Greek writers pictured the spirits of the dead in a "world below" as they waited for their time to be reborn. They described the spirits as looking—and often acting—just as they had in their living lives. However, as we come down to modern times we find very different ideas as to what the soul is like.

The Light in the Human Mind

Edward Bulwer-Lytton was a famed nineteenth-century author. He was also a serious student of the occult. Much of what he studied of the supernatural went into his books. Today he is remembered mainly for his famous novel *The Last Days of Pompeii.* But he wrote others, such as *Zanoni* and *A Strange Story.* Both are based upon supernatural themes.

In *A Strange Story*, a character uses a magic potion to enter the brain of a strange man he knew. This person was a very wicked man. As Bulwer-Lytton tells the story:

"The brain now opened to my sight, a labyrinth of cells. I seemed to have a clue to each winding in the maze. I saw therein a moral world, charred and ruined, as . . . the world of the moon is said to be."

He saw three kinds of light within the brain. One was red. Another was blue. The third was a silvery spark. The red light moved through the veins and nerves. The narrator decided that this red light was "the principle of animal life."

The blue light went through the entire body. It crossed and sometimes joined the red light, but always kept itself separate. This, he decided, was the "intellectual principle, directing the animal life, but not of it."

"But the silvery spark! . . . Its center seemed the brain. But I could fix it to no single organ. Wherever I looked through the system, it reflected itself as a star reflects itself upon the water."

He realized if all else in the body stopped, this silver light would continue to shine. He asked himself, "Can this starry spark speak the presence of the soul?" Then looking closer, he saw that the silvery light was not the soul, but was a halo around the soul.

A Machine to Talk with the Dead

Thomas A. Edison had his own idea of the soul. In October 1920, Edison startled the world by claiming in an article in the *American Magazine* that he had invented a machine by which the dead should be able to communicate with the living.

Edison was the inventor of the phonograph, the electric light bulb, the dynamo, and hundreds of other inventions. When a man like him spoke, the public listened with awe.

In the interview Edison said, "I have been at work for some time building an apparatus to see if it is possible for personalities which have left the earth to communicate with us.

"If this is ever accomplished, it will be done, not by any occult, mysterious or weird means, such are employed by so-called mediums, but by scientific methods," Edison added.

After this sensational interview appeared, *The Scientific American*, a leading technical journal, sent a reporter to find out if Edison really said what the *American Magazine* claimed.

The great inventor repeated what he told C. B. Forbes, who wrote the original article. He was working on such a machine. He went farther in this interview, giving his views on death.

At this time, spiritualism was strong in the country. Mediums claimed to talk with spirits through rapping noises and they sometimes made ghostly images appear at their séances.

Edison said that he did not believe in such spirits. However, he admitted that if there are no spirits there is nothing to carry one's personality and memories into a new life. Then there could be no reincarnation. Edison said that he did believe in the possibility of the rebirth of the human soul. Then what did he think carried the dead's personality and memory into a new life?

The article said: "Mr. Edison does not believe in the present theories of life and death. Just as he experimented with one substance after another in his search for the filament of the incandescent electric lamp, so he has searched and reasoned and built up a structure which represents his theories of what is life."

It turned out that Edison's idea of the soul was unlike anything we had heard before. He believed the human body was composed of billions of exceedingly tiny "entities" (things). These band together to form a person. They are within the body and operate and repair it but do not make up the body itself.

"The medical world has proved that the seat of our personality is in that part of the brain known as the fold of Broca. Now it is reasonable to suppose that the directing entities are located in that part of the body.

These entities, as a close-knit group, give us our mental impressions and our personalities."

He went on to say that "what we call death is simply the departure of these entities from our bodies." He thought that these entities swarmed together like bees. If they hold together after leaving a dead body, then the dead person's personality would survive. When the swarm enters a newly born body, then we would have reincarnation.

But if the swarm breaks up upon leaving the dying person, "then I very much fear," Edison said, "that our personality does not survive."

He ended the interview by saying, "I do hope that our personality survives."

Just because a man is famous and a great inventor does not necessarily mean that he is always right. What Edison said, like what Bulwer-Lytton wrote about and what Socrates taught, are only personal beliefs. There is no way to prove or disprove any of these ideas.

Importance of Studying All Ideas About the Soul

However, it is important to study all ideas about the soul. This is because there can be no reincarnation unless there is something like the soul that lives after we die. And which can carry the personality, thoughts, and memories that make us ourselves into a new body.

Therefore, the key to the secret of reincarnation lies in finding out what the soul really is, how it works, and how it would pass from one body into a newborn one.

Until we understand the secret of the soul, we are, in our study of reincarnation, like an amateur doctor trying to cure a disease. If a person has measles and we treat the spots on his body, we are only doctoring the symptoms (signs) of the disease. We have not touched the disease itself.

And it is the same in our studies of reincarnation. When we study déjà vu, use hypnotism to unearth Bridey Murphy, and amass case histories of people who seem to recall other lives, we are studying the symptoms or signs of reincarnation. These signs make us think there is such a thing as rebirth, but they do not prove it. The secret lies in the soul—whatever that will finally prove to be.

• 5 •

Hinduism and Rebirth

Iarchas the Indian has told us that his people taught reincarnation to the Egyptians. This may or may not be true. We have no way of knowing. But it is true that the ancestors of today's Indians brought a belief in reincarnation to Asia.

These ancient people called themselves *āryas*—a word that means "nobles" in their language. The Aryan language, by the way, is the root from which most European languages come.

These Aryan-speaking people began spreading over Europe sometime between 2500 B.C. and 1500 B.C. The tribes who would become the present-day Hindus of India came through the Khyber Pass between Afghanistan and Pakistan about 1500 B.C.

Here they found a great civilization with large cities located along the Indus River. The Indus rises in the Himalaya Mountains and runs through the center of Pakistan into the Arabian Sea.

These cities and the people who built them are one of the great mysteries of history. Until 1922 historians did not believe that any ancient people ever lived in the Indus valley. Then some workers accidentally uncovered evidence of a great city on the Indus River 200 miles north of Karachi, the capital of Sind, which is one of the four provinces of Pakistan.

This remarkable ruin is Mohenjo-Daro (Moh-henjoe Dare-oh), or "The Mound of the Dead." The city had been destroyed many times and new cities built upon the rubble of the old ones. Digging down through these levels, archaeologists found that the oldest level dated from about 2500 B.C.

Mohenjo-Daro was no collection of mud huts like so many ancient sites. It was carefully built of burnt bricks. A few stone heads and a tiny bronze dancing girl show that their art was developed.

Strange Writing

But most surprising of all, Mohenjo-Daro had a written language. Writing is believed to have begun in two places. One was in Sumer in the Middle East. This was cuneiform (wedge-shaped) writing. The other was the hieroglyphics (picture writing) of Egypt.

The writing of Mohenjo-Daro did not resemble either of these, although invented at about the same time. Cuneiform and hieroglyphics have been deciphered. The writing of Mohenjo-Daro is still a mystery. It does show that these people had attained a high degree of civilization.

The people of Mohenjo-Daro were no match for the invaders. The top level of the ruins shows marks of burning. Skeletons of people slain in the war were found in the streets when the ruins were uncovered.

The Mohenjo-Darans were driven out and the Aryans settled along the Indus. Their neighbors, the Persians, pronounced Indus with an "h," as Hindhu. They called the Aryans Hindhus, or people of the Indus River. This later became Hindu. Still later the "h" was dropped to create the word India by which the country is known today.

These early Hindus worshipped natural gods. And in nature we see constant rebirth. Plants grow, blossom, and die. But in the spring another green shoot appears. It grows, blossoms, and dies. We see the same thing in the animal world. In the den of the wolves, the burrow of the worms, in the tents of the nomads, and in the castles of the nobles, we see the cycle of birth, blossoming, and death. But in every case new life comes to replace the old. The gasps of the dying are balanced by the cries of the newly born.

Death is the end of life, but not the end of lives. Those who study nature see this constantly. It is easy to see how these early nature worshippers came to believe in reincarnation. Once one comes to believe in an eternal soul, it is easy to believe that this soul can come back in one of these new bodies.

The Vedas

The oldest religious writings in the world are the Hindu Vedas. These are beautiful hymns to the old gods of the *āryas*. The Vedas do not speak of reincarnation, although some scholars claim that there are hints of it. A later group of writings called the Upanishads (oo-PAN-i-shads) do set forth the Hindu ideas of rebirth. These writings make reincarnation an absolute part of the Hindu religion. Rebirth, in the Hindu belief, is something that must occur. There is nothing we can do to stop it until our souls are cleared of all sins.

Westerners often find Hinduism confusing. A Hindu may, for example, worship a hundred gods or one god. Yet he believes only in one god. This is possible because of Brahman. Brahman is the spirit of creation. All things come from Brahman. This includes the three main gods of Hindu worship. These are Brahma the creator, Vishnu the preserver, and Siva the destroyer.

The First Souls

The souls around which each human body grows were thrown off from Brahman like sparks from a bonfire. These first souls had wings and lived joyously in the skies of the earth. The earth, unfortunately, is a place of misery, sorrow, and sin. The souls became too much interested in the impure things of the earth. Thus they became impure themselves.

The souls came from Brahman and must return to Brahman to fulfill their destiny and achieve eternal happiness. However, Brahman is perfect. Being perfect, Brahman cannot be described. Earthly words are impure and the impure cannot be used to describe perfect purity. All we know is that Brahman always was and always will be. Brahman is neither male nor female. Brahman is not large or small, or young or old. Brahman is everything, for everything came from Brahman. Thus, although there are thousands of gods Hindus may worship, they really worship Brahman, no matter which god they choose.

It is both the duty and the desire of all souls to return to Brahman and enjoy eternal happiness. They cannot do so because the earthly impurities have tainted them. Only the absolutely pure may return to Brahman. Thus each soul must be purified. This is very difficult and cannot be done in a single lifetime. The soul must be reborn again and again until through good deeds and religious activity it becomes pure enough to return to Brahman.

The Wheel of Life

Hindus call this cycle of birth, death, and rebirth the "wheel of life." Their lives turn around and around like a wheel on an oxcart. Hopefully it moves a little bit forward with each turn.

The wheel of life is called *samsara*. When a person finally gains enough merit to escape from the cycle of rebirths, the release is called *moksha*. Then the freed spirit returns to Brahman.

Nirvana cannot be described, for it is a part of Brahman. And Brahman, we will recall, cannot be described by the impure words of earth. All agree, however, that the existence within Brahman is perfect happiness or bliss.

It can be seen then that Hindus do not look upon reincarnation as something to be hoped for, as Western believers do. Hindu rebirth is a punishment for an impure soul.

Rebirths will continue, Hinduism teaches, until the soul—through methods taught by the religion—cleanses itself. This is so difficult that many expect never to achieve it. All these people can hope for is to improve their lot in each life.

Hindus believe that the person, *thing*, or station in life of your next rebirth depends upon what you did in the life before it. In this way, one may be a beggar in this life and a king in the next. Or one may be a prince today and reborn as a dog or even as an insect.

There is a Hindu story of a fly that kept circling the statue of the god Siva. Siva looked upon this as a sign of the fly's religious devotion. So the fly was reborn in its next life as a great religious teacher.

This was not a reward. Neither is it punishment for

a wicked man to be reborn as a dog. It is just that each brought his new life upon himself by his own deeds in the life before.

Prisoners of Karma

The thing that determines what one will be reborn as is called *karma* (CAR-muh). Karma cannot be seen or felt, but it is real enough. It is made up of all the bad and good deeds of a person's life. If the good deeds outweigh the bad deeds, then one has a good karma. If one's bad deeds are more than the good ones, then the person has a bad karma.

This karma—formed from one's own actions entirely—controls the next life. A bad karma means a bad incarnation. A good karma means a good life. Then if a person ever builds a perfect karma, he or she can escape the wheel of life. There will be no more rebirths and the cleansed soul can return to Brahman.

From this we can see, in the Hindu belief, that one can control future rebirths only by doing as much good in the present life as possible.

I remember something that happened during my first visit to India more than twenty-five years ago. A beggar asked for alms. He looked half-starved and his clothes were in rags. I gave him a couple of small coins. Then I saw him cross the dusty street and give one to a crippled man.

"One of his relatives?" I asked my guide.

"Oh no," he replied. "He is seeking merit so he will not be reborn another beggar. Giving to one less fortunate than oneself is a way to gain merit and create a good karma."

I sincerely hope the ragged old man makes it.

You Can't Cheat Karma

There is a question Westerners often ask about karma. If a man is caught in a life of misery because of poor karma in his last life, can he kill himself and hope for a better life in the next incarnation?

Unfortunately, you cannot cheat your karma. The life you lead in each incarnation was designed by your karma in the last life. It is your fate and duty to live this life fully. It is the gravest of sins to end it before its natural end. If you do so, you will surely be reborn into a much worse situation than you had in the life you quitted by suicide.

Each person is a prisoner of his or her karma. One's only hope for a good life is to work for a good karma. So, the Hindu teachers tell you, make the best of whatever life your karma has earned for you, be it in a palace, a hovel, or the burrow of an insect or worm.

Transmigration

Transmigration means the movement of a soul to another body, and this is another word for reincarnation. However, it has come to mean chiefly the reincarnation of a human soul in an animal or an insect body.

This is an idea that Western thought has mainly rejected. The idea of a human being being reborn as a lower animal fills many with horror. The Greek philosopher Aristotle called the idea absurd. He said that a carpenter could not use the same tools as a musician. So, in a like manner, the human soul had to use the tools (body) for which it was intended.

On the other hand, Pythagoras, who did so much to introduce the idea of reincarnation to the Western world, did believe in transmigration. Many of those who hate the idea insist that Pythagoras never made any such claim, but a number of ancient writers claim that he did.

Some of these claims are jokes. In one of his plays, the Greek playwright Menander has a god ask an old man what kind of an animal he would like to be born as in his next life. The old man replied, "Let me be anything but a man, for man is the only creature who profits by injustice."

Plato (427?–347 B.C.) made several references to men being reborn as animals. On the other hand, Hierocles, who was a strong believer in Pythagoras, denied that his teacher really believed in human rebirth as animals. "He who believes that after death he shall put on the body of an animal is ignorant of the form of the human soul," he said.

How Belief in Transmigration May Have Started

Hierocles thought that when Pythagoras said men were reborn as animals in some cases, the great mathematician only meant that these people sometimes acted like animals.

Some think that Plato meant the same thing when he spoke of transmigration.

We often hear people speaking of others in animal terms. "He has a doglike manner . . . He is rat-faced . . . He reminds me of a snake . . ." There are actually people who do give the impression that they look like animals. Such resemblances could easily have inspired primitive people to believe such persons had been animals in a previous life.

St. Augustine voices an objection to transmigration in *The City of God.* He says that Porphyry "shrinks" from the idea of transmigration because "a woman who has become a mule might carry her own son on her back."

All we can say about transmigration is that it, like so many other things in the broad subject of reincarnation, has neither been proven nor disproven.

We must remember that five hundred and twenty-four million Hindu people believe in transmigration. It is taught as part of their religion. With these people it is a matter of faith. None of us has any right to condemn another's religion and faith until we study it thoroughly.

Gods Who Come Back

Hinduism teaches that human beings are not the only creatures who can reincarnate. The gods may do so too. This is voluntary, of course, and only done to help mankind.

Vishnu the preserver is the most loving of the Hindu gods, and the one who comes back to earth the most often. A god reborn in human form to help mankind is called an *avatar*. There are hundreds of avatars of Vishnu. Each has the name by which he was known in his earthly rebirth. Krishna is the most beloved of all Vishnu's avatars.

This Is Where It Started

There is much in the Indian beliefs in reincarnation that Westerners do not agree with. They argue against transmigration of souls into animals. They refuse to accept the idea of karma. They find the idea of Brahman conflicts with their own religions. And so on.

However, a study of India's beliefs is important to any study of rebirth because it was in India that the theory of reincarnation was born.

• 6 •

The Lives of the Buddha

In 563 B.C. a child was born to the family of an Indian ruler of a small kingdom. The child's name was Siddhartha, and in time he became the Buddha, founder of a religion that today has about 250 million followers.

At the time of the boy's birth, a fortuneteller said that he would leave his home when he found out about sorrow, sickness, and death. His father, not wanting to lose his son, gave orders that none should tell the boy of these things. A special palace was built for him. It had everything he could desire, so the prince would never have to go outside where he might learn of sorrow, sickness, and death.

However, one day the prince did leave the palace. He saw a sorrowful old man. Later he saw a sick man. Then he saw a dead man. In this way he learned of sorrow, sickness, and death. True to the prophecy, he left home to take up the life of a homeless religious wanderer.

The Buddha's Search

The future Buddha was a very devout Hindu in those days. He followed all the rules and almost starved himself to death to purify his soul. Yet he never found the religious peace he sought. After six years of searching he decided that Hinduism was wrong. He developed his own ideas, taking part of Hinduism and adding changes of his own to make what today is called Buddhism.

The Buddha agreed with Hinduism that the world is a place of misery and sorrow. He also accepted the idea of rebirth and the wheel of life. He agreed that human beings are ruled by karma and that karma is the result of one's good and bad deeds.

He agreed that happiness could only come if one is released from the cycle of rebirths. But at this point his ideas broke away from Hinduism.

Hindus believe the soul, once it is purified, returns to Brahman and there finds eternal bliss. Buddha preached that there were no gods at all and no Brahman creator spirit to return to. Even more startling, he taught that there are no souls.

In the Buddha's beliefs, karma takes the place of the human soul. This karma, the sum of our good and bad deeds, is the only thing that remains after we die. The human body is made of earth, water, fire, and wind. As soon as the body dies, the karma is released. It immediately draws to itself more earth, water, fire, and wind to create a new body for the next rebirth.

As in Hinduism, karma controls what each person becomes in this new body.

Enlightenment

The Buddha believed that people could escape from the wheel of life through meditation (deep religious thought) and by following the Eightfold Path. This is a list of eight things that govern a Buddhist's actions. When these things have been done, a person becomes enlightened. All desire for worldly things ceases. The cycle of rebirths cease, and the person can enter nirvana.

The Buddha never described nirvana, although his followers often asked him about it. So no one really knows what nirvana is. Some have called it an actual place. Others think that it is only a state of mind. In any event, the results are the same as when a Hindu achieves moksha and rejoins his soul with Brahman. In nirvana a person escapes the misery of being reincarnated again and again. From this point on, he or she enjoys eternal happiness and bliss.

Buddha and Karma

The Buddha agreed with Hinduism that karma is a force created by a person's good and bad deeds. He also agreed that karma determines the kind of life a reincarnated person will have in his or her next rebirth. He also agreed that a person can escape future rebirths by following certain religious rules and principles.

Buddha differed with Hinduism over how a person could find salvation and escape the wheel of life. Each person, Buddha taught, must find the way within himself through profound meditation, thus becoming "enlightened."

He also differed in rejecting the idea of the human soul. The body decays and is lost upon death. Only one's karma remains. This karma then attracts new elements to itself and a new body is formed. The question then is, can this new body really be called the reincarnation of the old personality?

A Buddhist sermon answered this question thusly:

"Walk down to the river and watch the water flowing past. The water moves between the banks of this river, moving from its source to the sea.

"Tomorrow go back and again look at the flowing water. It is the same river as it was yesterday. We see the same banks, the same trees, the same grass. But the *water* flowing between these banks is not the same water of yesterday. That water has already flowed to the sea.

"This is new water we see today. It is not the water of yesterday. And this water we see now is not the water we will see if we come back tomorrow. It is new water, but can you honestly say that the river itself has changed? So it is with our many lives. Karma is the banks of the river of our lives. All else is water flowing past the banks."

Memories of Other Lives

In the Western idea of reincarnation, memories, personality, and whatever it is that makes us ourselves are carried from one life to the other by the soul. Karma also carries these things that make a person himself or herself.

The Buddha was able to remember every one of his hundreds of past lives. These have been collected in a book known as the *Jataka* (rebirth) *Tales*. They do not tell the whole story of each life, but only an incident from each. These were related by the Buddha as lessons to his followers.

In one of the *Jataka Tales*, the Buddha was walking in the jungle when he came upon a starving tigress with seven small cubs. She had been ill and was too weak to hunt. The Buddha sacrificed his life so she could eat him and regain strength to hunt for her family.

In another life, the Buddha told how he was walking along and stopped to smell a flower. A fairy angrily accused him of stealing the smell of the flower, for he had not asked permission to take it. The Buddha agreed that he was a thief. He promised that he would never again take anything without first asking permission.

In the 500 *Jataka Tales* that have been collected, the Buddha is shown in every walk of life from a king to a beggar to an animal.

Transmigration

Buddhists, like Hindus, believe in transmigration. A person, depending upon his karma, may be reborn in animal or insect form.

For this reason, some Buddhist sects refuse to kill any living thing. They will not even swat a fly or a mosquito.

"These are living things," they say.

Just as the Buddha showed in the Jataka tale of the stolen smell, an insignificent theft is as great a sin as a large theft. So the killing of an insect is as great a stain on one's karma as the killing of a man.

Reincarnation of the World

The original religion taught by Buddha was a very simple way of life. After his death Buddhism split into many creeds with different ideas. Some of these came about in order to answer questions that came up. Some expanded ideas that the Buddha only touched on. Some were made to fit changing conditions of the times.

When people became more educated, they wanted to know more about how creation started. Although the Buddha did not believe in gods, in some creeds he himself was made a god.

In one account, written long after the Buddha's death, there is a story of how the world was formed, how it will die of old age in the same way a person dies, and how it will be reborn, just as people follow the wheel of life.

This story says that originally there was only water. Then land formed in the great ocean. The only life consisted of beings made of light, who were survivors of the death of the previous world. These beings were sinless and pure. Then they began eating the things they found growing in the new lands that arose from the water.

They began to crave these earthly things. This brought about sorrow, sickness, and death—the three things that the Buddha's princely father tried to shield his son from. The creatures of light became men, trapped by the wheel of life. They were thus doomed to undergo continual rebirths upon the earth until they could overcome their karmas and reach enlightenment.

Time, in this account, is measured in *kalpas*. The Buddha explained the kalpa in this manner:

"Go to the largest of all mountains in the world. Wipe it with a soft cloth. This great mountain will be worn away by the rubbing before one kalpa shall have passed."

The Three Periods of a Kalpa

A kalpa is divided into four periods of time. The end of the first period is when the beings of light lose their spiritual qualities. They fall from grace and become prisoners of an earthly karma, doomed to continual rebirth until they free themselves.

The second period is our present time. It is a time of misery and suffering with sorrow, sickness, and death for all of us.

In the third period the world begins to dissolve and is destroyed in the fourth period to end the kalpa. The total kalpa covers billions of years.

But this is not the end. The world is reincarnated and a new kalpa begins with a time of water and darkness. This is followed by the formation of land, which corrupts the spiritual creatures who were purified and survived the destruction of the world in the last kalpa.

This goes on and on. It is described in Buddhist writing that each kalpa follows the other as the waves of the sea follow each other.

A person can escape his or her cycle of rebirths and find eternal happiness in nirvana. But apparently the world is doomed to be reborn forever.

Past Memories

Many of the case histories collected to support reincarnation have come from India. Dr. Ian Stevenson, the most noted investigator of reincarnation, included quite a number in his writings.

Many of these case histories of other lives came from children. This is thought to be logical. A child is closer to his former life than an older person. His or her mind has not had time to become cluttered with memories of the present life. Therefore, memories of the last life should be more clear.

Stories gathered from such Indian children are not accepted without something to support them. Parents are questioned. So are people who lived where the reincarnated person is supposed to have lived in this other life. Then if the child's memories are of things that really happened, and which he or she could not have known about in this life, it is assumed that this person is truly one who has been born again.

This type of proof can only be gathered in the case of a child who was reincarnated very soon after its death in the other life. This ensures that there are people still alive who can remember incidents to support the memory of the reincarnated person.

Dr. Chari's Caution

Dr. C. T. K. Chari, a professor at the university at Madras, India, cautioned against accepting such case histories without very careful checking. He pointed out that the majority of Indians believe in reincarnation. He thinks that this surely affects the evidence in many cases. He said, "India's 'pro' attitude toward reincarnation beliefs may unconsciously influence the testimony of parents and interested bystanders."

In other words, those who believe deeply in reincarnation are poor witnesses. No doubt this is true. However, there are cases where the evidence is so strong that it puzzles even those who doubt.

The Memories of Shanti Devi

One of the most famous cases is that of a little Hindu girl named Shanti Devi. This quiet, thoughtful child was born in Delhi, the capital of India, in 1926. She first began talking of her past life when she was three, describing the "other home" where she lived.

Her memories increased as she grew older. She claimed to have been born in 1902 in her last life. She married a man who sold cloth, and had one son before her death. They lived in the village of Muttra, eighty miles from Delhi.

She had a strong desire to see her old home and kept begging her parents to take her back. Finally an uncle told her that if she could recall the name of her husband he would take her back to Muttra for a visit.

Shanti Devi named Kedar Nath Chaubey. Her relatives were startled to learn that a person by that name still lived in Muttra. A letter was sent to him. He replied that he had had a wife whose name had been Ludgi, which was the name Shanti Devi had given as her own in her other life. Kedar Nath said that

Ludgi died in 1924—two years before Shanti Devi was born—or if you believe her story, reborn—in 1926.

The Visit to Muttra

Shortly after this Kedar Nath visited Delhi. When Shanti Devi saw him she recognized him as her husband in the other life, although she had never seen him in this one. He talked to her, asking questions that would have been known only to his dead wife. Shanti Devi answered correctly in each case.

Kedar Nath told her parents that he was convinced that the eleven-year-old girl had been his wife in her other life.

After this, Shanti Devi kept begging her parents to take her to Muttra. They finally agreed to do so. They had never been happy about their daughter's memories of her past life. There was a belief in India at that time that children who recalled other incarnations did not live long.

In Muttra the eleven-year-old girl knew every street and place of interest. Her parents insisted that she had never been there in this life. They knew of no one, including themselves, who might have told her about the place.

Now all of this was certainly enough to establish a good case for this being a true case of reincarnation. However, something even more startling was to come.

The Lost Money

They went to a temple in Siva where Shanti Devi said she once worshipped. The sight of the temple awoke new memories. The girl recalled that in her other life she had saved money to make a gift to the temple. She had hidden the money in a hole in the corner of a room in the house of her husband.

They went to Kedar Nath's house and asked him to look in the room. An odd expression passed over the man's face. He took them inside the house and showed them a hole under a loose board. The hole was empty. Shanti Devi's hidden money was gone.

"I found it after my wife died," he said.

Kedar Nath swore that he had never told anyone about finding his wife's secret hiding place.

Word of this quickly got around, and a large group of people came and asked Shanti Devi's parents to leave her with them. The parents refused, although the girl was willing to stay.

Her father insisted that the girl's death wiped out all obligations to her old life. Her good karma had caused her to be born as his daughter. She was his in this life, and he would not share her with those who knew her in another life.

The Investigation

The story of Shanti Devi created wide interest. A committee made up of a newspaper editor, a politician, and a lawyer investigated the facts in the case. It was their opinion that this was one of the most remarkable cases of reincarnated memory they had ever heard of. Even those who did not believe in reincarnation could not explain how the girl even knew about the hiding place of the money. Perhaps, they said, she can read minds.

Shanti Devi, at last reports, is still alive. However, her memories of her other life have grown dim, and she now refuses to talk about them at all.

• 7 •

The Fourteenth Incarnation

The question is often asked, "How do we know that a person is truly reincarnated? Isn't there some proof besides a few memories, which often cannot be checked?"

The most serious and profound attempts to prove that a person had been reborn were made by the lamas, or Buddhist priests, of Tibet. Here it was not just curiosity or an attempt to prove or disprove the idea of reincarnation itself.

Until the Chinese took over Tibet in 1959, the country was ruled by a god-king who was believed to be the reincarnation of the Tibetan god Chenrezi. There have been fourteen of these reincarnations. Each has been known as the Dalai Lama (DAH-lie LAH-muh). The fourteenth Dalai Lama is now living in exile in India, after fleeing Tibet in 1959.

The Tibetan religion is a form of Buddhism that incorporates some of the magical elements of the old pagan religions. This religion teaches that when a Dalai Lama dies he is immediately reborn into the body of a child somewhere in Tibet.

The Search for the God-Child

The Dalai Lama does not marry. There is no direct line of blood through which his soul can carry. The rebirth of his soul may be in any part of the country and in any level of society. It is the duty of the high lamas of the religion to find this child, provide him with proper religious instruction, and to place him upon the throne of his country.

This is no light duty, for these searchers seek both a king and a god. If there is the least doubt about their choice, then both the political and spiritual welfare of the country is endangered.

The thirteenth Dalai Lama, a very great man, died in 1933. Immediately the search began for his reincarnation. Foreign observers who were in Tibet at the time have left accounts of how this search was made. In addition, the fourteenth Dalai Lama wrote the story of his life, a book published in 1962. These accounts tell us exactly how the search was made and what convinced the searchers that a two-year-old peasant boy was the fourteenth reincarnation of the Dalai Lama.

The dying lama could not tell his followers where he would be reborn. There would be signs and the lamas would have to interpret these as clues in the search for the reborn god-king.

The Sacred Signs

The first sign, on the day of his death, was some curious cloud formations seen from Lhasa, the capital of Tibet. These clouds appeared in the northeast. They towered higher than usual and moved in an odd way, as if they were trying to form the image of a person—an image that never quite became clear.

A single sign might be an accident, not a true sign. This one indicated that the child might be found in the northeast of Tibet. But more signs would be necessary to prove it and to show in what part of the vast northeast section this might be.

Immediately after his death, the thirteenth Dalai Lama's body was embalmed and placed on a throne in his summer palace. This was so that the faithful could come and pay their last respects to one who had been like a father to his people. After a few days the awed lamas noticed that the dead man's head had turned. It had been facing south. Now it looked to the northeast.

At the same time fungi grew in a star shape on a pillar of the palace. This mark was upon the northeast side.

These signs were submitted to high government officials, lamas trained in the finer points of reincarnation, and to those trained in magical rites. All agreed that these were true signs.

But where in the northeast? Northeastern Tibet

stretched to Tsinghai, more than a thousand miles away. This distant province bordered on China and was claimed by the Chinese government as its territory.

Other signs were found, studied, and accepted or rejected. Finally, after two years of search and study, the regent who ruled Tibet until a Dalai Lama could be found went to a sacred lake ninety miles from Lhasa.

Pictures in the Lake

This lake is Lhamoi Latso. There are underwater currents in the lake. These cause different reflections and movements that seem to form images deep in the water. For centuries Tibetans had believed that these dim pictures in the lake foretold future events.

The regent took his place on a high hill where he could see the full expanse of the sacred lake. He prayed, meditated, watched, and waited. Then sometimes he would go down to the shore and peer closely at the waters.

He came away with the feeling that he had seen some dim pictures in the water. These visions were written down in secret. This was done so that none but himself and three close advisers would know what the signs were. The signs were then tested among the lamas and astrologers without their knowing what the signs were.

According to Dalai Lama's autobiography, "The regent saw the vision of three Tibetan letters—*Ah, Ka,* and *Ma*—followed by a picture of a monastery with roofs of jade green and gold, and a house with turquoise tiles."

For the next year lamas were sent out looking for such a monastery with a nearby house that had a turquoise-blue roof. A monastery with the required green and gold roofs was found near the village of Taktser in the district of Amdo in Tsinghai province, in the area disputed by China and Tibet. This monastery was called Kumbum. Near it on another hill above Taktser was the monastery of Karma Rolpai Dorje. The thirteenth Dalai Lama had once stayed at the second monastery while returning from a visit to China.

The three advisers responsible for reading the signs decided that the letter *Ah* seen in the lake by the regent stood for Amdo. *Ka* could mean the monastery of Kumbum. Or *Ka* and *Ma* combined might stand for Karma in Karma Rolpai Dorje. Both monasteries fit the description of the one seen in the lake vision by the regent.

The question now was: Can the vision be fulfilled by finding a private house with a turquoise roof?

The House of the Blue Tiles

An official party of searchers came to the village. They talked to the head lama of Kumbum monastery. He told them that there was a house with a turquoise tile roof in the village.

"Are there young children in this house?" the lama in charge of the searchers asked.

He was told that there were several children in the family. The youngest was a boy born about two years before this. This would be the right age. With the other signs pointing the way, Lama Kewtsang Rimpoché, the leader, decided to see the boy.

First he gathered all the information he could about the child. The boy was considered very intelligent. Although barely two years old, he was already helping with the family chores. One of these was gathering eggs from the hens the family kept. He was quite playful. Once he crawled into the nest and tried to cackle like a hen who had laid an egg.

Before going to the house with the blue tile roof, the Lama Kewtsang Rimpoché dressed in poor clothing. His assistant put on better quality material, acting the part of the leader, but Kewtsang behaved as a servant. They claimed to be wandering monks on their way to Lhasa. They asked at the house of the blue tiles for food and a place to stay for the night.

Both men closely observed the two-year-old boy during this short visit. They were greatly impressed and were pleased when they left because the child begged to go with them.

The two searchers reported back to the full group. They agreed that up to this point the signs pointed to this house and this boy. In addition, they were told by the monks from the local monastery that the thirteenth Dalai Lama had passed by the house with the turquoise roof on his return from China. At the time the Great One had remarked that it was a pretty house.

The family had not recognized the first two seekers, but when the full company came they knew then that their son was being considered as the reincarnation of some great man. However, they did not dream that it was the Dalai Lama. The abbot of a local monastery had recently died. They thought it was he who was reincarnated in their son.

The Tibetans believe that young people, because they are closer to their previous life than older persons, keep some of their memories of other lives. These memories are dim, of course. You rarely find a Tibetan who claims to recall details of his other lives. However, young children will often recall some object they used in a previous life.

The Tests for Reincarnation

The seekers brought with them two rosaries of black beads. One of these had belonged to the dead Dalai Lama. The other had been especially made to look exactly like it for use in these tests.

The rosaries were placed on the floor in the room with the child. He was more interested in the visitors than in the religious objects. But after a while he turned to them. The seekers watched. Their faces were impassive, but all admitted later to strain and anxiety.

The boy passed the false rosary and picked up the one that had belonged to the dead Dalai Lama. He fingered the beads and then slipped them over his head.

The seekers concealed their feelings. They repeated the test, but used yellow rosaries this time. Again the boy chose the correct one.

The child could have accidentally made the correct choices. So the next test was deliberately designed to fool him. Two drums were brought out. One was small and rather plain. It had been used by the dead Dalai Lama to call his attendants when he wanted them. The second drum was larger and beautifully decorated. It was expected to appeal to the normal two-year-old more than the small plain drum.

However, the boy chose the small drum and began to beat upon it. Although the seekers continued to keep their faces straight, their excitement was growing.

They prepared for the final test. If the boy passed this, they would report to the regent in Lhasa that they thought the new Dalai Lama had been found.

The False Stick

Two black wood walking sticks were laid on the floor. As with the other objects, one had belonged to the dead man. The child picked up the other one. Some of the seekers could not keep the disappointment from showing in their faces. It had been two years since the Dalai Lama died, and they were impatient to find his successor.

The child's actions were curious. He seemed puzzled and put down the false stick. Then he picked up the other one.

This confused the seekers. Their mission was to find the true Dalai Lama's incarnation. A mistake on their part would be terrible. It would not only put a false god-king on the political and religious throne, but would be a terrible injustice to the real Dalai Lama. They could not take any chances. They withdrew to consider this new turn of affairs.

Why had the child picked the wrong stick and then changed his mind? Until they knew the answer to this, the seekers would not certify the boy as the true incarnation they sought. The wrong stick belonged to one of the group. He was asked where he got it. He replied that it had come from another lama. One of the others remembered this man. He had been given a walking stick by the old Dalai Lama and in turn had given it to a friend.

It would appear from this that the stick the boy first chose had really been owned for a short time by the Dalai Lama. This accounted for the boy's puzzlement when he picked it up and for him dropping it to pick up the other. This showed that the boy was more sensitive than they had imagined. His picking up both sticks was hailed as stronger proof that he was indeed the reincarnation they sought.

In the Hearts of the Seekers

There was one final test. The boy did not take part in this. It went on in the hearts of the seekers. All the signs pointed to this child being the reincarnation of the god-king. He had successfully passed the tests put to him.

Now the final test was for each seeker to ask himself this all-important question: "How do I feel in my heart about this child? Is he really my god and my king?"

In making a selection as important as this, there is no place for doubt. Each seeker searched his heart. After long meditation and prayer they all agreed: "This child is indeed the fourteenth Dalai Lama, god-king of Tibet."

This section of the country was then under Chinese control. The Chinese governor refused to let the seekers take the child to Lhasa. It was 1940 before this trouble could be resolved and the new Dalai Lama taken to the Tibetan capital and proclaimed the reincarnation of the dead lama. He then had to undergo years of religious training.

Another Tibetan Reincarnation

There is another account of a Tibetan search for a reincarnated person. This is told by Rato Khyongla Nawang Losang in his book, *My Life and Lives*.

According to Khyongla (pronounced Chungla), he was five years old in 1928. At this time four monks on horses rode up to where he was playing beside an irrigation ditch. They gave him presents and rode away after promising to see him again.

The Strange Signs

Later the boy's family was told that their son was believed to be the reincarnation of Khyongla, an abbot who had directed a famous monastery, by means of rebirths, since 1510.

Before Rato was born his mother dreamed that some gods appeared and poured water on her head. She told friends about this and asked them what it meant. Another time she dreamed that the sun and moon came together. Then on the day that the baby was born a rainbow appeared. Those who saw it from a distance said that one end seemed to touch the boy's house.

These signs were reported to the monks at the monastery. They were greatly interested because the boy's house was west of them. When the old abbot Khyongla was cremated, the smoke from his funeral pyre drifted to the west.

Two other boys were found and the signs of all three were placed before an old monk who was thought to be an oracle. He went into a trance and picked Rato. This still was not considered final proof. So a complete account of the signs was written in a report and sent to the thirteenth Dalai Lama, who was still alive at this time. He verified that Rato was indeed the reincarnation of Khyongla.

Finding Reincarnated Family Members

Of course it is only people in positions of importance who are sought in this manner. The ordinary folk are aware that they have lived before and will live again, but few know or care what they were in the past life. When a beloved family member dies, those left behind sometimes try to find out what became of him or her. They rarely succeed, for villages are widely scattered and people do not have the opportunity to travel.

In his autobiography the Dalai Lama told about the reincarnation of his baby brother. His family came with him to Lhasa. In time his mother gave birth to another girl and a boy. The boy died when he was two years old. He had been greatly beloved, and they were all deeply grieved by his death.

Astrologers had to be consulted as to the right day for the baby's cremation. The family was surprised to be told that the baby should neither be cremated or buried. The body should be embalmed and then the child would be reborn in the same house. This was done and butter was smeared on the dead child's body to make a small mark.

Later the Dalai Lama's mother gave birth to another son. The Dalai Lama wrote in his book: "A pale mark was seen on the spot on his body where the butter had been smeared. He was the same being, born again in a new body to start his life afresh."

• 8 •

Judaism, Christianity, and Rebirth

Today neither Judaism nor Christianity accepts reincarnation. This has not always been so. At different times in history there were strong believers in both religions.

According to both religions people have but one chance to redeem themselves of their sins. If they fail to do this in their lifetime, the opportunity is lost forever. Many religionists say this is a good thing. If we have other lives in which we can correct and redeem the sins of this one, then there is no pressure upon people to be just, devout, and god-fearing in their present lives. There is danger of people saying, "We can atone in a later life."

The Bible and Rebirth

One of the strongest arguments both Jewish and Christian opponents of reincarnation use is that the Bible does not tell us that people have many lives.

Here again we run into disagreement. Those who support rebirth say that the Bible does speak of reincarnation. Edgar Cayce, the famous psychic, once said that he could show you references to reincarnation in the Bible, but that someone else could show you that there are none. This is because many passages in the Bible are written in such a way that one person can understand it one way and another will see the meaning in an exactly opposite way.

One of these Biblical passages is Ecclesiastes, first chapter. We are first told that these are "the words of the Preacher, the son of David, king in Jerusalem." This would appear that it is Solomon speaking.

We are first reminded that life goes on. One generation of people follows another. The sun also rises, goes down, and rises again. The wind blows first from the north and then from the south. All rivers run down to the sea, but the sea is not full, for the waters (through rain) return to the place they came from.

Then in the ninth verse: "The thing that hath been, it is *that* which shall be; and that which is done *is* that which shall be done; and *there is* no new *thing* under the sun.

"10. Is there *any* thing whereof it may be said, See, this *is* new? it hath been already of old time, which was before us.

"11. *There is* no rememberance of former *things*; neither shall there be *any* rememberance of *things* that are to come with *those* that shall come after."

Those who believe in reincarnation see in these

verses a clear statement of their ideas. The Preacher is speaking of the human soul. He is telling us that it is like the sun, which sets, rises, and sets to rise again. The soul is like the river, which runs to the sea, turns to rain, and flows into the river to run again to the sea.

Again, when the Preacher speaks of there being nothing new under the sun, the argument is that he was speaking of the soul as well as of all other things. Later in chapter four (4:16) he says, "*There is* no end of all the people, *even* of all that have been before them . . ." (Emphasis added.)

Those who do not believe in reincarnation say that not one word in these passages mentions rebirth of the soul into a new body. What the Preacher is saying is that new life comes to take the place of that which dies.

In a similar manner there are a number of places in the Bible that some see as hints of reincarnation, even if rebirth itself is not mentioned. All of these have been disputed.

Reincarnation and the Jews of Biblical Times

Reincarnation is not mentioned by name in the Old Testament. Regardless, there are passages that indicate that some Jewish people of Biblical times may have believed in it.

Two passages are often pointed out to support this

claim. One is in the Old Testament and one is in the New Testament (King James Version). In Malachi (4:5), the last book of the Old Testament, is this declaration: "Behold, I will send you Elijah the prophet before the coming of the great and dreadful day of the Lord."

Elijah lived in the days following Solomon, about five hundred years before Christ. During these years, the belief persisted that Elijah would return to earth. In Matthew 16:13–14, Jesus asked his disciples: "Whom do men say that I the son of Man am?" The answer was, "Some say that thou art John the Baptist; some Elias; and others, Jeremiah, or one of the prophets."

Elias is the Greek rendering of Elijah.

In this reply to Christ, many investigators see proof that the people of Biblical times believed that the old prophets at least could be reincarnated. We also find that Herod the king believed reincarnation possible. When he heard of Jesus Herod asked if this could be John the Baptist reborn. Herod had earlier executed John.

There are those who claim that Jesus's own words prove reincarnation. They base this claim on Matthew 17:12. Jesus has again been asked about the coming of Elias. He replied: "But I say unto you, that Elias is come already, and they knew him not."

Many of those who do not believe the Bible speaks of reincarnation do not deny that this statement of Christ's clearly says that Elias did return to earth after his death. However, they say that he was sent back by

God—in whom all things are possible—to help humankind, not because he had to come back under force of his karma. This was a special case and does nothing to prove that the rest of us can or must return for another life—unless God individually wills it.

Such opinions of what the Bible says are just that—opinions. One can find a lot of written arguments about this, but after reading it and the quotations given, we can only say neither side has proven its case.

The Beliefs of the Essenes

The Jewish historian Flavius Josephus lived in Roman times in the Holy Land. He wrote two very famous books that have survived to this day, *The Jewish War* and *The Antiquities of the Jews.*

In those times there were three major Jewish schools of thought. Two of these groups, the Pharisees and the Essenes, believed in reincarnation, according to Josephus. But the Pharisees, he wrote, "Say . . . that the souls of good men only are removed to other bodies. The souls of bad men are subject to eternal punishment."

Josephus wrote a lot about the Essenes. They believed that the human soul was drawn out of the air "and united to their bodies as to prisons, into which they are drawn by natural means."

The Essenes are best known today as the writers of the famous Dead Sea Scrolls. These are ancient copies of the Old Testament found in caves near the Dead Sea in 1947.

The Cabala

The *Cabala* appears under different names. Some spell it Kabala. Others put it Kabbalah. There are even those who begin the word with the letter Q.

In any event, it comes from the Hebrew word *kabbal,* which means "to receive." Some say that Cabala, used as the title of writings, means "that which has been received" or "tradition."

We have noted how both those who believe in reincarnation and those who do not argue over the true meaning of certain passages in the Bible. The Cabalists go beyond this and argue that there is a secret meaning in the Bible understood only by those learned in the mysteries of the Cabala.

The Cabalistic writings, based upon and explaining this hidden Biblical wisdom, are supposed to have started with Moses. They were passed down orally until put in writing around the third century B.C. The Cabala was put in its final form in medieval times.

The Cabala is filled with magic and mystical writing, covering many fields. It is difficult to read and more difficult to understand. However, we are concerned here only with what the Cabala has to say about reincarnation.

This is stated very clearly. In one section it is said

that there are 613 precepts (commandments) that a religious person must observe. No one is perfect unless he or she keeps all of these commandments. Any person who fails to keep these rules of religious conduct "is doomed to undergo transmigration once or more than once until he observes all he had neglected to do in his former life or lives."

Transmigration in this case means rebirth into another body, rather than into animal or insect form as the term is more generally defined today.

This statement from the Cabala sounds almost as if it came directly from Hinduism.

The Zohar

Even more like Hinduism is a passage from the *Zohar*. This Cabalistic writing was begun by a rabbi in A.D. 80 and was expanded by others in the thirteenth century.

In one passage the *Zohar* says positively that all souls are subject to rebirth. No one knows how many times this must happen "or what mysterious trials" the soul must undergo in being reborn.

The *Zohar* goes on to say that every soul must reenter the absolute thing that they came from. We presume this absolute thing is either God or heaven. This return cannot be made until the souls are perfect. If the souls cannot reach perfection in one life, then "they must commence another, a third, and so forth, until they acquire the perfection which fits them for reunion with God."

If we did not know we were reading from a Jewish book, it would seem like we were recounting a Hindu explanation of release from the wheel of life to rejoin Brahman.

The Wide Belief in Reincarnation

These accounts of Jewish belief in reincarnation in earlier times are not mentioned to support those who claim that rebirth is told in obscure passages of the Bible.

I have included them here merely to show that regardless of whether the Bible mentions or does not mention reincarnation, many people of Biblical and medieval times believed in it.

Early Christians, as well as Jews, also believed in rebirth, even though Christianity as a whole rejects reincarnation today.

Beliefs of the Early Saints

Many of the early saints of the Catholic church believed in reincarnation. St. Augustine (A.D. 354–430) was one of these. St. Augustine belonged to a pagan cult before he was converted to Christianity. One of his duties in this cult was to teach reincarnation. He kept this belief in rebirth even after he became the Christian Bishop of Hippo (a place in North Africa).

We find this belief in his famous *Confessions* in which he wrote: "Did I not live in another body, or somewhere else, before entering my mother's womb?"

St. Jerome was mainly responsible for the *Vulgate*, the Latin translation of the Bible. According to Manly Palmer Hall, St. Jerome (A.D. 340–425), "declared that the doctrine of transmigration was taught as an esoteric mystery in the early Church." This esoteric (secret) knowledge was given only to a few selected people.

Gregory of Nyssa, father of the Greek church, believed, "It is necessary that the soul be healed and purified. If this does not take place during its life on earth, it must be done in future lives."

Statements like this one lead to disputes. Those who believe in reincarnation see it as a clear proof of their beliefs. Those who do not believe say that Gregory said only "must be done in future lives." Nothing was said about these lives being upon the earth. These may be different stages of a spiritual life—in heaven, in hell or some other stage between earth and heaven.

So the fruitless argument goes on. The strong belief in reincarnation during the time of these early Church saints came from Neoplatonism. This was a philosophy that developed in Alexandria, Egypt, in the third century A.D. It came about from a new interest in Plato and the old Greek philosophers. Plato, of course, was a strong believer in rebirth.

The Neoplatonists (the new Platonists) tried to combine points from Plato with points common to

Judaism, Christianity, and the mysticism of the Near East.

Origen

The single person who had the most to do with spreading a belief in reincarnation in the early Church was Origen. This famous Christian teacher and writer lived in Alexandria. His time is in doubt, but is thought to have been from A.D. 185 to 254.

In *Contra Celsum*, Origen said, "Is it not reasonable that every soul for some mysterious reasons (I speak now according to the opinion of Pythagoras and Plato) is introduced into a body, and introduced according to its deserts and former actions?"

This statement is pure Hinduism.

Origen's writings had great influence for almost 200 years. Then some Church leaders began to criticize Origen. In the sixth century Emperor Justinian of the Eastern Roman Empire began a struggle with Pope Vigilius for control of the Church. This led to a council held at Constantinople in A.D. 553. Vigilius didn't want to attend because the emperor invited only those bishops who favored his own beliefs. Although the teachings of Origen were not the major issue, the council condemned them. In the end, the pope had to agree.

• 9 •

Some Who Believed

The most famous name among modern people who have believed in reincarnation is that of Edgar Cayce. Cayce has a remarkable reputation among psychic people.

Reincarnation plays only a small part in Cayce's psychic work, which was revealed when he was in trances. In fact, we are told that Cayce was surprised himself when reincarnation began to show up in the readings he gave for people who came to see him.

Later the psychic readings he gave were more and more involved with the former lives of people who sought his help. Some of these "life readings," as he called them, go back to Atlantis, the legendary island that is supposed to have sunk in the Atlantic Ocean some time around 9,000 B.C.

The Psychic Healer

Edgar Cayce first came to fame as a psychic healer. He did not practice medicine himself, for this would have been illegal. However, while in trances he could diagnose difficult medical problems and suggest appropriate treatment

This strange ability came to the attention of a medical doctor who used Cayce's suggestions. Cayce continued this work until his death in 1945. The records of his successes are amazing. However, we are not concerned with them, but with his work in reincarnation.

All of Cayce's readings were taken down by a secretary and are on file at the Association for Research and Enlightenment, Virginia Beach, Virginia. This is a nonprofit organization headed by Cayce's son, Hugh Lynn Cayce. Interested people are permitted to inspect these records.

There are 14,246 readings in the Cayce file. Twenty-five hundred of these are called "life readings." In the life readings, Cayce gave accounts of each subject's past lives. In many cases events in these lives were shown to influence the subject's actions in this life.

How Life Readings Were Made

In the case of Joan Grant's far memory, some object triggered the woman's recollections of other lives. In the case of Bridey Murphy, hypnotism was used to unlock deeply buried memories of past lives. The method Cayce used was totally different. He told the subject what the person's past lives had been.

Cayce agreed with the theory that the human mind holds in its subconscious memories of its past lives. What he did in his trance was to tap into these subconscious memories. In this way he could bring forth information that the person's own mind could not recall.

In a talk he gave in 1933, Cayce, said that he knew very little about how he was able to do this. In fact, he said that more than one thing was working for him in reaching back into his subjects' past lives.

In connection with tapping the subconscious, which we mentioned above, Cayce said, "One source, apparently, is the record made by each individual in all of its experiences in what we call time. The sum total of these experiences is written, so to speak, in the subconscious of that individual."

Tuning in on the Akashic Records

Cayce also claimed another unusual ability beyond being able to tune in on the subconscious mind of his subjects. This is tuning in on the "Akashic Records."

Akasha, the source root of Akashic, is a Sanskrit word. Sanskrit is the language in which the ancient Hindu sacred Vedas were written. The theory is that Akasha is a substance of atomic thinness that covers the entire universe.

Everything that happens, whether an action, spoken word, or thought, is recorded upon the Akasha, according to this belief. This makes the Akashic Records one giant cosmic tape recording of all that has ever happened.

How can actions and even thoughts be preserved like this? We do not know that they are. But if they are, and if you must have a "scientific" explanation before you will consider the idea, here is a way it might be done.

All things give off radiations of some kind. The only difference between radiations is their wavelengths. Light is a radiation. So are radio waves. Heat from a stove and from the sun are radiations too.

The human brain also gives off radiations. These are called encephalographic waves (brain waves). They can be measured and recorded to give graphs.

A tape recorder turns words into electromagnetic waves, which can impress themselves upon magnetic tape. The tape can then be replayed to recreate the original sounds.

In a like manner, we can theorize that the many radiations of people, things, words, and thoughts impress themselves upon the Akasha to create similar permanent records.

Cayce said, "Anyone may read these records if he can attune himself rightly. Apparently I am one of the few people who can lay aside the personality sufficiently to allow the soul to make this contact to the universal source of knowledge."

Cayce went on to say that he did not believe that he had any power that the rest of us did not have. It is all a matter of setting your own mind aside so that your soul can tune in on the—so to speak—soul of the universe.

Cayce could not do this when awake. He had to be in a self-induced hypnotic trance. This removed his own personality and thoughts from the business at hand. With his own consciousness drugged by sleep, his "soul mind" could then contact the subconscious memories of his subject or read the impressions left by this person on the Akashic Records.

This is Cayce's explanation of how he could determine what people did in their other lives. We can accept it or reject it. There is no way of proving the accuracy of what he says happened in Atlantis or ancient Rome or during any of the other remote times. All we can do is look at Cayce's other accomplishments—and some of them are remarkable—and then decide if we want to believe him or not.

Cayce and Karma

Edgar Cayce believed in karma. He believed that many of the illnesses of those who came to him for help were the result of something they had done in an earlier life on earth. He believed that when the soul enters a new body an opportunity is immediately open for it to redeem itself for past sins.

Sometimes this happens without a person knowing about it. Then she might say, "I guess my luck has changed." But Cayce says that it was not luck at all. "It is the result of what the soul has done about its opportunity for redemption."

Cayce believed that illnesses were the result of sins and often these sins were committed in previous lives. One case involved a thirteen-year-old girl who suffered from epilepsy. No treatment helped her for long.

Cayce did a life reading for the girl. He found that she had the same parents today that she had had in another life during colonial times. Cayce said, in his trance reading, that the girl's trouble came from things she had done in the American Revolutionary War.

Then he added that her parents must share the blame. The family had sided with the British in the struggle for American independence. They forced the girl to spy for the British. It was not so much the spying that ruined her karma as it was the sinful things she did to get her secret information.

The Girl From Atlantis

This was not the only source of the girl's trouble. Reading deeper into the Akashic Records, Cayce discovered that she had once been the daughter of Atlanteans who fled to Egypt when their island home sank in the ocean.

As she grew up, the Atlantean girl worked in a hospital where she had no sympathy for the sick.

In between this life in Egypt and her spying in the American Revolution, the girl had led a sinful life in the Holy Land. All of these things had left their mark upon her character, leading to her current illness.

Paying Our Debts

In such readings Cayce seemed to be following the old Hindu laws of karma, but there is a major difference. Cayce believed that one's own free will was stronger than karma, and that it did not take forever to work off a poor karma. Cayce was a deeply religious man who made it a point to read the entire Bible at least once each year. However, he never agreed with the Christian belief that relief from one's sins is accomplished through prayer. He believed each person must work out payment through direct actions, but that God is merciful and will help.

I personally find Cayce's life readings not convincing. However, I have mentioned them here because so many people disagree with me, and also because of Cayce's great reputation in other psychic fields.

His views on tuning in on the subconscious of his subjects and on the Akashic Records are interesting. They are also possible, although there is no proof of Akashic Records. If there is such a thing, then it should be possible to devise a machine to tune in on them. This would be along the lines that Thomas A. Edison was working on with his machine to talk with the dead. If an electromagnetic force exists upon which all records of actions, sights, talks, and thoughts are impressed by electromagnetic waves, then a machine to tune in on them is perfectly possible.

It is doubtful, however, that anyone—regardless of

his genius—could build such a receiver until he first discovered exactly what Akasha is. Nobody has done that yet.

Reincarnation as a Medical Aid

Edgar Cayce is not the only person who used memories of the past to cure or help people in physical misery today. Denys Kelsey, a British psychiatrist, has done extensive work in this field. Kelsey told about some of his cases and his beliefs in a book called *Many Mansions*. This book was written with his wife, Joan Grant. Ms. Grant, you will recall from Chapter 2, is the famous author of *Winged Pharaoh* and other books in which she remembers her other lives.

Dr. Kelsey had been using hypnotism in his regular psychiatric practice. At first he put his patients in a hypnotic trance to help them recall forgotten incidents that might be the cause of their mental trouble.

Later, with the help of Joan Grant, he began pushing his patients' memories beyond this life to lives in other times and places. In this he was doing precisely the same thing that Morey Bernstein did with Bridey Murphy. However, Bernstein was seeking to prove reincarnation itself. Kelsey, like Cayce before him, was probing for incidents in former lives that might be the source of mental or physical illnesses in this life.

While his basic purpose was the same that Edgar

Cayce's had been, his method was different. Cayce used his own psychic powers to read his patient's subconscious memories. Kelsey used hypnotism to force the patient's subconscious mind to recall its own past.

Daydreams of Long Ago

Kelsey relates a very curious case from one of his earlier attempts to send a male patient's mind back to a former life. The recollections were short flashes in which a lovely young lady appeared.

The scenes the patient described changed constantly. It might be compared to a montage of scenes from a movie. One moment she was on a yacht and then the scene abruptly changed and she was at Ascot, a famous race track in England. In a similar manner she was seen at other famous places. Usually she was with a handsome escort. There was no connection between any of the hurried scenes.

Joan Grant, who was helping with these hypnotic trance sessions for the patient, had more experience with recalling past lives than her husband, the doctor.

According to Dr. Kelsey's report, Ms. Grant recognized these scenes as being true recall of a past incarnation. However, she said that none of them actually happened. The male patient that they were treating had been this young woman in a past incarnation. This is nothing unusual. Those who study rebirth are generally agreed that a person may be reborn anywhere in any kind of body, of either sex or of any race.

The incidents that the hypnotically sleeping patient was recalling were not things that actually happened, but were daydreams and fantasies of this woman of yesterday.

Living in a Dream World

Doctors often meet people who live in dream worlds. Beset by troubles in their everyday, unhappy lives, these people retreat into their own dream world. In these fantasies they see themselves as they would like to be. Psychiatrists call this a retreat from reality.

All of us indulge in dreams of this type at one time or another. The dangerous daydreamers are those who retreat so far into their dream worlds that they lose touch with the real world. They live constantly in their make-believe world and it becomes real to them. They often get to the point where they cannot tell their dream world from the real world.

The young man that Kelsey treated had been such a person in his earlier life as a girl in England. Digging deeper into this other incarnation, Kelsey found that this girl came from a poor family. She fell in love with a young man from a higher station. This proved to be a tragic affair, leading to the girl's death.

Subconscious memories of this life were so scarring that they affected the young man's present life. This produced the nervousness and anxiety that brought him to the psychiatrist in the first place.

Once this was understood, then a cure was possible. It was only a matter of getting the patient to understand what his trouble was and that what happened in his last life was not his fault.

Dreams or Reality?

I have brought up this case of Dr. Kelsey's because it illustrates a very important point in studying claims of past incarnations.

Time and again investigators have reported on the sincerity of those they studied.

"They cannot be frauds," we are told.

And we must admit that the accounts were real enough to those who told them. But would they be real to the rest of us? How many of these are recollections of past daydreams?

And also, how many of the accounts were deliberately changed by the teller? This was suggested in the famous case of Bridey Murphy. Bridey said her father was a lawyer. No record of any such lawyer could be found. It was suggested that Bridey was ashamed of her father's real, low position in life and deliberately tried to make him more important. We find this happening in the world of today and there is no reason to believe that it cannot happen with those recollecting past lives. A liar in one life does not necessarily become a truthful person in the next ones.

Dishonest Spirits

Spiritualists have often been embarrassed by spirit actions that have been at times dishonest and at other times too playful.

E. W. Capron, an early spiritualist, and others have explained this in the following manner:

"Just because a person died, he or she does not immediately become all-wise, all-knowing, and all-good. If a person's personality survives death—and personality means those traits of character that makes a person the individual person he or she is—then this person's ghost will have the same traits as the living.

"A foolish person will make a foolish ghost. A criminal person will make a criminal ghost. A wise person may make a wise spirit. In any case, advice received through spirit mediums and means should be carefully considered in light of the spirit's character and background."

The same can be said of people recalling their past lives. There are hypnotists who claim that a subject cannot lie under hypnosis. Bridey Murphy would suggest otherwise. Dr. Kelsey's patient was not lying. It was mental confusion between reality and fantasy, but still it was an untruth.

It is reasonably possible that some of these claims of past incarnations, dredged up by hypnosis, are true. But how can we tell the true ones—if there be such—from the false and the honestly mistaken?

In Search of Reality

In the case of Dr. Kelsey's patient, Ms. Grant spotted the unreality of the patient's recollections of a young woman in some famous settings.

Ms. Grant, from her own experience in reincarnation, told how she was able to spot these accounts as fantasies or daydreams instead of actual happenings.

She said this was because there was no action. The person was just there in a famous place. This was because the girl had never been in any of these places. She could picture herself there, but could not picture herself doing anything. She did not know what to do.

I am not sure that such a test would work in all cases. Sometimes daydreams are built upon stories or motion pictures that people have seen or tales they were told. One of the most difficult tasks in studying case histories of reincarnation is trying to eliminate such false "memories."

An investigator who has tried perhaps the hardest of anyone to do this is Dr. Ian Stevenson, the foremost scientific explorer of reincarnation we have today.

● *10* ●

Searching for the Truth

Dr. Ian Stevenson has been associated with the University of Virginia School of Medicine for many years. Dr. Stevenson was born in Canada in 1918. He studied medicine and was associated with the Alton Ochsner Medical Foundation in New Orleans, Cornell Medical College, and the Louisiana State University School of Medicine before joining the University of Virginia School of Medicine.

Dr. Stevenson is a psychiatrist and his work, dealing as it does with so much abnormality of the human mind, led him into parapsychology. His work first aroused notice in 1960 when he won an essay contest held in honor of William James, the pioneer psychologist. Dr. Stevenson's winning essay was called "The Evidence for Survival from Claimed Memories of Former Incarnations."

Then in 1966 the American Society for Psychical Research published Dr. Stevenson's book, *Twenty Cases Suggestive of Reincarnation.* This has become the most highly regarded book ever written on the subject of rebirth. In the bibliography for *The Mysteries of Reincarnation,* Daniel Cohen called it "the only reincarnation book around with any claim to scientific accuracy."

In his famous book, Dr. Stevenson reported on cases he had personally investigated. In every case he did not depend upon what someone told him. He talked to the person and those who knew this person. He visited the scenes of the supposed reincarnation and applied all he knew of psychiatric interviewing.

One of Dr. Stevenson's cases that has aroused great interest is that of a five-year-old boy in Lebanon. A surprising number of Stevenson's cases involve young people. This seems to bear out the claims that memories of past incarnations are strongest in childhood and grow dimmer with age.

Imrad Who Was Ibrahim

The child's name was Imrad Elawar. He lived in Kornayel, a village near Beirut, the capital of Lebanon. Stevenson heard about Imrad while in Lebanon on another case. There were some unusual things about the case that aroused the doctor's interest.

He went to Kornayel and talked to both the boy and his father. Imrad first began to talk about having another life when he was two years old. He claimed that his family name had been Bouhamzy. He had lived in the village of Khriby.

Khriby was fifteen miles from Kornayel, but there were mountains between the two places. A road connected them but it was so twisted that the road distance was twenty-five miles. It was a difficult trip and few made it unless it was necessary.

When Imrad was four he suddenly left his grandmother, who was caring for him, and ran up to a stranger in the street. He claimed the man had once been his neighbor.

As it happened, the man was from the village of Khriby. Imrad's father questioned the visitor. This man said, in answer to the questions, that there was a family named Bouhamzy living in Khriby.

Stevenson learned from Imrad's father the following important points:

1. Imrad often spoke of Jamile and how pretty she had been.
2. He often used the name Mahmoud, but when asked about it the boy could not explain what the name meant to him.
3. He once spoke of an accident in which a man's legs had been crushed. The man later died.
4. He spoke of a dear friend he once had.
5. He often said that he was glad that he could walk.
6. There was also something about a truck accident.

These recollections were only bits and pieces. The boy could not hold a long train of thought about them, nor could he connect them.

But from these Imrad's father told Stevenson that he believed that his son was the reincarnation of Mahmoud Bouhamzy, who had lived in the village of Khriby. The man who became his son in this other life had been married to a woman named Jamile. Mahmoud Bouhamzy had both legs broken in a truck accident and died as a result of his wounds. The memory of this tragedy was what caused the boy to speak often of how wonderful it was to be able to walk.

Another Side of the Story

This is a very reasonable explanation that ties all the loose ends of Imrad's bits of memories into a life story. Unfortunately, the life story did not hold up under investigation. However, a different one came to light in a manner that shows that one cannot rely on the obvious when investigating the mysteries of reincarnation.

A Mahmoud Bouhamzy lived in Khriby, but he was still alive. However, he had a relative named Said Bouhamzy who had been killed in a truck accident two years before Imrad was born in Kornayel village.

Said did not have a wife named Jamile. There were other things Imrad had said that did not tie in with Said's life.

At this point many researchers would have given up. It was obvious that Imrad's claim to being the reincarnation of a Bouhamzy was not true.

Still it is curious that a two-year-old should have told such a story. If he had been making up a fantasy, it would have seemed more likely he would have made himself someone important. In the majority of documented cases of reincarnation claims, the subject does claim to have been a king or queen or someone of great importance. One investigator claimed that he knew five different people who claimed they could prove they were once Marie Antoinette, Queen of France, which would have required Marie's shade to have split into five parts.

Still Another Bouhamzy

Stevenson did not give up. He kept digging and uncovered still another Bouhamzy. This man was Ibrahim Bouhamzy, a cousin of Said, who was killed in a truck accident. Ibrahim had lived with a woman named Jamile. Ibrahim had been a dear friend of Said Bouhamzy, his cousin, who was killed in the automobile wreck. This wreck happened in 1943.

Ibrahim died himself in 1949. He developed spinal trouble. This made it impossible for him to walk during the final two months of his life.

The facts of Ibrahim's life more closely fit the pieces of Imrad's memories than any of the others. In addition, those who knew Ibrahim said that he had a vicious temper. Imrad also was given to high rages. So in character as well as events, Ibrahim fit the role of Imrad in another life.

Ibrahim's Life

How could Imrad have gotten mixed up as to which Bouhamzy he was? As Stevenson unraveled the story, Imrad had not gotten mixed up at all. His recollections were unconnected pieces. He recalled the name Bouhamzy. He remembered a beautiful woman named Jamile. He mentioned a truck wreck that killed a man after breaking this man's legs. He also recalled not being able to walk himself.

But at no time did the boy ever say that he was Said Bouhamzy. He never said that he had a wife named Jamile. He did not say that *he* was killed in a truck accident or that his legs were broken.

He had memories of these things and his father was the one who tried to piece out the story by assuming that these things had happened to his son. Actually most of these things happened to his son's dear friend in another life. They made such an impression on the man Ibrahim that he carried the memories over into his next incarnation.

Memories of a House

An investigator who only seeks information to support his case is a false researcher. It is necessary to look for things against as well as for, if one wants a true picture. It is also important because if you don't somebody else will. This is what happened in the case of Bridey Murphy. Those who do not believe in reincarnation and Bridey Murphy in particular brought up many damaging objections. These have cast doubt on the entire case—without, of course, really proving it wrong.

Stevenson does not make this mistake. He investigated the negative and the positive aspects of Imrad's story. For one thing, when he took Imrad and the boy's father to Khriby, the child did not do well at all in recognizing things in the village. He did not even know the direction to his supposed house.

However, in the house itself Imrad showed an amazing knowledge. He pointed out the place where the goats had been kept fifteen years before he was born. He did the same with a tool storage place, as well as with fourteen other separate items.

Stevenson also considered the possibility of fraud, that the boy's parents were fooling him. But this did not seem to be the case. They had nothing to gain. Reincarnation is a common belief among these people. There was nothing for them in either honor or money in trying to trick the doctor.

He also considered the possibility that Imrad had heard people talking about the Bouhamzy family and had woven what he heard into childhood fantasies.

Stevenson talked to a number of people in both villages. They agreed that there were very few visits between the two places. The road was hard to climb and they did not have much business with each other.

Also, Imrad was only two years old and just beginning to talk when he first claimed to be the Bouhamzy man. Ibrahim was hardly a man a child would choose as a hero, even if Imrad had known him. He was always quarreling and once shot a man during a fight. There were also other things about Ibrahim that were not admirable.

A Strong Case

In a brief sketch like this it is not possible to go into all of Stevenson's evidence. However, those who have studied the case and compared it to others claim that this is one of the strongest cases ever presented for true reincarnation.

As the title of his book clearly sets forth, Dr. Stevenson does not claim that this is a true case of rebirth. The book is called *Twenty Cases Suggestive of Reincarnation.* The key word here is "suggestive." There is no doubt about it. The case of Imrad *suggests* that the boy may have been the reincarnation of Ibrahim Bouhamzy.

Such highly suggestive cases give us confidence to dig deeper into this most fascinating study.

The Total Recall of Edward Ryall

In 1974 a book called *Second Time Around* by Edward Ryall was published in England. The following year it was published in the United States as *Born Twice.*

The author, like Joan Grant, claimed to have total recall of a previous life. According to Ryall's story, he had been a farmer in England in 1685. This is the time that the Duke of Monmouth led a revolt against his uncle, James II. Monmouth was the illegitimate son of King Charles II. As such, he could not inherit his father's throne. So when Charles died, the crown of England went to his brother James. James was believed to be a Catholic. Monmouth used this as an excuse to rebel. He said he was upholding the Protestant faith of the Church of England.

The rebellion was short-lived. It ended with Monmouth's defeat in the battle of Sedgemoor. Ryall claimed to have been killed in the early stages of this battle.

Ryall had these memories since childhood in his present life. However, he never mentioned them to anyone. He feared people would think him crazy. Then in 1970 the *Daily Express,* a London newspaper, invited its readers to send in accounts of their previous lives.

After much thought, Ryall decided to send in something about his life in the time of Monmouth. The newspaper selected four letters from the hundreds received. Ryall's account was one of those chosen. It created wide interest because of its apparent sincerity. There was a ring of truth about it that impressed those who read it.

Dr. Stevenson's Opinion of Ryall

Ryall's story in the British newspaper was brought to Dr. Stevenson's attention. He wrote to Mr. Ryall and later visited him in England. Still later, the two wrote to each other. The letters were so numerous that Stevenson said they filled two large files.

Then when Ryall wrote his book, Dr. Stevenson contributed both an introduction and an appendix to it. In the introduction Dr. Stevenson tells why he believes that Ryall's story is true.

He said that when investigating a case of this kind he first tries to explain it by normal means. Only when all of these fail does he consider reincarnation as the true explanation.

In the case of Ryall's account, he considered the possibility of fraud. He rejected this idea. Some people have suggested that telepathy, mind reading, or second sight may be behind these so-called far memories. Stevenson considered this explanation and rejected it also. There was no one whose mind Ryall may have subconsciously read. In fact, if such could be proven, it would be almost as great a discovery as reincarnation itself.

He also considered the possibility of ancestral memories. This theory holds that memory may be inherited the same way one inherits blue eyes, or brown hair, or any of various family traits. This was a possibility, but there was no evidence that would support it.

After considering these and other possibilities, Dr. Stevenson wrote: "This brings me to say therefore that, as of now, I believe it [Ryall's story] best interpreted as an instance of reincarnation. In other words, I think it most probable that he has memories of a real previous life. . . ."

Checking on Details

Dr. Stevenson's appendix to Ryall's book shows how deeply he investigates a case. It contains a listing of thirty-one scholarly books he consulted to check on details of seventeenth-century English life as related by Ryall.

To those who might doubt his story, Ryall, on the title page of his book, printed this quotation from Voltaire, the great French writer:

> *After all, it is no more surprising to be born twice than it is to be born once.*

● II ●

Tomorrow and Tomorrow and Tomorrow

In their search for proof of reincarnation, most investigators work only with the memories of those who claim to have other lives.

This, admittedly, is a poor way to proceed. Memories are faulty. They can be misinterpreted, just as Imrad's parents drew incorrect conclusions from the fragments of their son's memories. They can be the result of delusions, hypnotic dreams, ancestral memory, or even plain fraud.

Unfortunately, we have no real way of separating one from the other. As a result, accounts of previous incarnations are rarely convincing.

It would help if we could find people in different parts of the world—who could not possibly have had contact in this age and time—who recalled similar experiences in a past age. I knew a man once who worked on this.

In Search of Old Friends

This man had a job that required much world travel. He had been in more than half the countries of the world. He and I met in India when he overheard me questioning a boy I had for a guide. I was asking the boy, who was about fourteen, about his memories of other lives.

I was getting quite a fanciful tale, which I suspect was just something to please a tourist, in hope of a big tip. It did serve to bring me into contact with this man, whom I will call John Smith.

In the talks that followed between this man and me, he spoke of his beliefs about rebirth. He had some very vivid memories of his own past lives. He never said what they were, for they were to be part of tests he wanted to conduct.

His idea was that somewhere in the world there are people who shared these former incarnations with him. If they did not actually meet, then they at least shared a common adventure. For example, both may have been at Yorktown when George Washington defeated Lord Cornwallis to win the American Revolutionary War.

If two such people could recall incidents that were identical, but which are not found in history books, he felt this would be a strong argument for reincarnation.

He did not go around asking if anyone had helped George Washington in a previous life or any of the

other historical incidents that he believed himself to
have been in. This would have opened the way for
fraud. Instead, he relied upon what he called a "human déjà vu." In other words, he felt that when he
met a person he had known or seen in another life he
would have the typical déjà vu feeling of having done
this before.

He admitted to me that only twice in his life had he
experienced the feeling of having known a particular
person in another life. In both cases he did not reveal
this to the other person. Instead he brought the conversation around to the period of time he felt they
had been together or associated in some manner.

In one case he could arouse no answering interest
in the person with whom he talked. The person
showed no interest at all in the period of time my
acquaintance discussed.

A Reminder of Something Forgotten

In another case his talk of a particular time did arouse
a very interesting reaction. The other person listened
with intense interest. At one point he said with a puzzled air, "What you say reminds me of something. I
don't know what it is. It seems like I am about to
remember something and then it fades away on me."

This conversation occurred during an Aegean Sea
cruise to the Greek islands of Crete, Rhodes, and San-
torini. During the four-day voyage, the investigator

talked to this person several times. He was never again able to arouse another flicker of interest.

While he agreed with me that this could be a coincidence, he insisted that it was sufficiently encouraging to make him want to continue.

I have often wondered how he made out.

I also have the feeling that he was trying to feel me out as well. I had mentioned that I had been in India years before as a soldier. This got him talking about soldiering, for he had also been in the military service at one time.

Then for what seemed no really good reason to me, he got to talking about soldiering in the Revolutionary War. If he was trying to probe me, it was not successful. He struck no familiar chord.

Finding Life's Secrets in Death

A doctor I talked with briefly one afternoon during a tour of Persepolis, the ancient ruins in Iran (Persia), told me:

"I do not believe that reincarnation can ever be proven or disproven by studying memories people claim to have of their former lives. I think it would be much more profitable to seek the secret of reincarnation by studying death."

His reasoning was that the soul is the key to reincarnation. We do not yet know what the soul really is.

Nor do we know where the soul resides while awaiting its new birth.

In the case of the Dalai Lama, the Tibetan belief is that he is immediately reincarnated. The soul leaves the dead body and flies directly to a new one. In the case of Edward Ryall, it was 217 years before he was born again after dying at Sedgemoor. Imrad, the Lebanese boy, was fifteen years in being reborn after he died as Ibrahim. And so on.

Where does the soul reside until it is reborn? There are many opinions. They range from different kinds of heavens and hells to a simple gray world that is little better than nothingness. There is no agreement on this.

Others claim that the soul stays in the grave until it is recalled. Those people who believe in ghosts and spirits think the spirits haunt old houses and castles.

For a long time death has been a taboo subject that people do not like to think about. In recent years this unnatural fear of death has been changing. More and more responsible investigators are trying to find out what death really is. Their work—whether scientific, spiritualist, or religious—is an important step forward in the study of reincarnation as well. If they can prove the soul scientifically and show how it leaves the body and where it goes, we are in a good position to continue and find out how it comes back.

The best work in the study of death has come from Dr. Raymond A. Moody and the pioneering Dr. Elisabeth Kübler-Ross. Both have made extensive interviews with patients who have been "clinically dead" and then were revived.

Reviving the Dead

We often hear of cases where a person's heart stops beating. The patient is then revived by heart massage, life support machines, or doses of strong drugs. What do these people see, feel, or think during the time they may have been dead?

These are the kinds of people Moody interviewed. We can give the same objections to such interviews as we do to memories dredged up by hypnosis. How do we know that these are real and not delusions brought on by a sick mind? And certainly anyone who has "died" must be sick in mind and in body.

In such cases we can only compare different stories to see if they agree.

And there does seem to be some agreement. In his book *Life After Life,* Dr. Moody reports that a number of people he interviewed claimed to have left their bodies. They seemed to see it from a distance. They felt peaceful. A number claimed to see a being of light toward which they were drawn. This was not a brilliant light, but it emitted warmth and love.

Religious people associated the light with Jesus Christ, but it was reported by both religious and non-religious people who were revived after being considered dead.

Separate World of the Suicide

Those who were revived after trying to kill themselves sometimes had a different story. A number interviewed by Dr. Moody (reported in his second book) spoke of seeing a gray world. There were people in it, but they walked aimlessly around. None of them, however, said they were disturbed by this gray world they found themselves in.

While the presence of the being of light, noted in Dr. Moody's first book, indicates the possibility of heaven, he said that no one described anything that suggested hell.

Professor Kenneth Ring of the University of Connecticut echoed Dr. Moody in some points. He too said that both religious and nonreligious people reported much the same thing.

Ring made a study of one hundred people who had been revived after being considered dead. He found that half of these remembered nothing of what happened while they were supposedly dead. Those who did report having visions told stories very close to those Dr. Moody reported.

Work of this type has been denounced by some as "Satan inspired," or as pure delusions. However, the fact that different investigators in different sections of the country are getting similar results argues for their accuracy.

The important thing about such work is that it does point a way to help prove or disprove the theory of reincarnation. If they prove that a *conscious* soul remains after death, then reincarnation at least becomes possible. Then if we can trace the soul as it leaves the body, we may in time find means of following it on to either its next rebirth or its final resting place.

If there is a soul, then it can be detected *by the proper means*—whatever these prove to be. We lack today the intelligence to find these means. But fortunately there is always a new generation coming along with new ideas. If they can't do it tomorrow, then there is always another tomorrow and still more after that.

In Search of the Soul

Spiritualism has sought to communicate with the dead through people called mediums. The theory here is that the physical powers of spirits are too weak for them to make direct contact with the living. Mediums, according to spiritualism, are those peculiar people who have the power—lacking in the rest of us—to help spirits make this contact.

Thomas A. Edison, with his experiments, was trying to find a mechanical means of doing the same thing.

Spiritualism has been so riddled with fraud through the years that it is difficult to tell what it has accomplished. Louis Elbé, in a book published in France in 1905, has some interesting things to say about the soul. If he is right, then our future incarnations—if any—could be different from those of the past.

He said that spirit communications, which pretend to come from beyond the grave, have never shed any light upon the problem of future life.

"Even if we admit the immediate survival of consciousness," Elbé said, "we are bound to recognize that it must undergo a radical change. This is owing to the mere fact of its separation from the physical body."

He pointed out that changes go on in the present time but are so small that we do not notice them. But totalled they "acquire an importance impossible to foresee."

An old man near the end of his life has been different types of persons during his long lifetime.

"Even so the mother, who, after long years of separation, finds her loved son once more in her arms, is bound to recognize that he is no longer the child she remembers.

"If life, then, changes the consciousness, how much more profound must be the transformation ensuing upon death."

In other words, if experience changes us during our lifetime, what changes will occur in our soul from the experiences between death and the time of rebirth?

This could mean that a person's character, desires, and even morals may be grossly different from those of the person who died.

This change could come about through such things as the manner of a person's death. A person who had a difficult time and starved to death could emerge resentful of society.

A man who had an unfortunate love affair and killed himself could very well emerge with a twisted soul. And so on through many possibilities. Elbé is merely arguing that experiences in death and after death could affect the soul's mental and moral outlook. If this is true, then it would change the person's character in his next rebirth.

Is It Really Me?

In such cases, we can ask, "Would such a person really be *me*?" I suppose the answer would be: "Yes, you are you." After all, changes in our living life did not cause us to stop being ourselves. Certainly none of us have the same outlook at twenty that we had when we were ten. And a man of sixty has changed very much both in body and mind from what he was at twenty. This may be why Mohandas K. Gandhi, the great Indian patriot and a strong believer in reincarnation, wrote:

> *It is nature's kindness that we do not remember past births. Where is the good either of knowing in detail the numberless births we have gone through? Life would be a burden if we carried such a tremendous load of memories. A wise man deliberately forgets many things. . . . Yes, "death is but a sleep and a forgetting."*

Seeking Our Roots

It is hard to argue with a man of Gandhi's stature. However, offsetting his view is that of Henry Ford, who did see a great advantage in recalling the experience of past lives.

It is the nature of the human race to want to know about its roots. We see this in the strong interest in history and in the enormous amount of time people spend in genealogical studies.

If reincarnation could ever be proven to be a fact, and if a method could be devised for stimulating any dormant memories of our past lives, might it not add immeasurably to our experience level? Would it cut the time needed for education? For example, if we could recall algebra lessons of a previous life, it would not be necessary to study them again in this or future lives.

It would revolutionize the study of history. It would also go a long way toward proving or disproving some religious theories—and possibly point the way to a universal religion. It would ease the fears of the future, and help us understand the nature of mankind.

None of the so-called proofs of reincarnation are real proofs. They are enough, however, to keep us seeking for other and better proofs. We must keep in mind that while nobody has proven that reincarnation is a fact, neither has anybody proven that it isn't. We must each look at the evidence or lack of it and make up our own minds.

"When You Were a Tadpole . . ."

From the time the human race first conceived of a soul and the possibility that it could be reborn until the present time, there have been many theories, ideas, and accounts of reincarnation. In this century the most popular of them all has not been a scholarly account, a personal story, or a general argument. It turns out that the most popular account is a poem written by a newspaperman in 1895. Nobody claims that it is great poetry, although Edwin Markham, the famous poet author of "The Man With the Hoe," saw fit to reprint this poem of rebirth in an anthology of poetry he collected.

The poem is called "Evolution" and was written by Langdon Smith. It first appeared in the *New York Herald* in 1895. Some years later Smith rewrote it and added additional verses. The revised poem was printed in an 1899 issue of the *New York Morning Journal*.

The poem was so popular that the Frank A. Munsey Company reprinted it in *The Scrapbook,* a magazine, in 1906, and then reprinted it again in 1908. After that, it appeared in book editions of four different publishers over the years, as well as in various anthologies. In 1941, a science fiction magazine reprinted it, and the latest printing I know of was in 1965 in *The Best* magazine.

In the poem there are many geological terms such as Cambrian, Caradoc, Kimmeridge, Purbeck, Coraline, and the like. These refer either to geological periods or to locations where evidence of past life was found. Delmonico's, mentioned in the last part of the poem, was a famous restaurant in New York in the 1890s.

This is Langdon Smith's poem, in which so many people for the last eighty years have seen their idea of reincarnation pictured as they would like it to be:

> *When you were a tadpole and I was a fish,*
> *In the Paleozoic time,*
> *And side by side on the ebbing tide*
> *We sprawled through the ooze and slime,*
> *Or skittered with many a caudal flip*
> *Through the depths of the Cambrian fen,*
> *My heart was rife with the joy of life,*
> *For I loved you even then.*
>
> *Mindless we lived and mindless we loved,*
> *And mindless at last we died;*

And deep in a rift of the Caradoc drift
  We slumbered side by side.
The world turned on in the lathe of time,
  The hot lands heaved amain,
Till we caught our breath from the womb of death,
  And crept into light again.

We were amphibians, scaled and tailed,
  And drab as a dead man's hand;
We coiled at ease 'neath the dripping trees,
  Or trailed through the mud and sand,
Croaking and blind, with our three-clawed feet
  Writing a language dumb,
With never a spark in the empty dark
  To hint of a life to come.

Yet happy we lived, and happy we loved,
  And happy we died once more;
Our forms were rolled in the clinging mold
  Of a Neocomian shore.
The eons came, and the eons fled,
  And the sleep that wrapped us fast
Was riven away in a newer day,
  And the night of death was past.

Then light and swift through the jungle trees
  We swung in our airy flight,
Or breathed in the balms of the fronded palms
  In the hush of the moonless nights.
And, oh! what beautiful years were these,
  When our hearts clung each to each;

When life was filled, and our senses thrilled
In the first faint dawn of speech.

Thus life by life, and love by love,
We passed through the cycles strange,
And breath by breath, and death by death,
We followed the chain of change.
Till there came a time in the law of life
When over the nursing sod
The shadows broke, and the soul awoke
In a strange, dim dream of God.

I was thewed like an Auroch bull,
And tusked like the great Cave Bear;
And you, my sweet, from head to feet,
Were gowned in your glorious hair.
Deep in the gloom of a fireless cave,
When night fell over the plain,
And the moon hung red o'er the river bed,
We mumbled the bones of the slain.

I flaked a flint to a cutting edge,
And shaped it with brutish craft;
I broke a shank from the woodland dank,
And fitted it, head and haft.
Then I hid me close to the reedy tarn,
Where the Mammoth came to drink—
Through brawn and bone I drave the stone,
And slew him on the brink.

I carved that fight on a reindeer bone,
And with rude and hairy hand;

I pictured his fall on the cavern wall
That men might understand.
For we lived by blood, and the right of might,
Ere human laws were drawn,
And the Age of Sin did not begin
Till our brutal tusks were gone.

And that was a million years ago
In a time that no man knows;
Yet here tonight in the mellow light,
We sit at Delmonico's.
Your eyes are deep as the Devon Springs,
Your hair is as black as jet;
Your years are few, your life is new,
Your soul untried, and yet—

Our trail is on the Kimmeridge clay,
And the scarp of the Purbeck flags;
We have left our bones in the Bagshot stones,
And deep in the Coraline crags.
Our love is old, our lives are old,
And death shall come again;
Should it come today, what man may say,
We shall not live again?

God wrought our souls from the Tremadoc beds,
And furnished them wings to fly;
He sowed our spawn in the world's dim dawn,
And I know that it shall not die.
Though cities have sprung above the graves
Where the crooked-boned men made war,

And the ox-wain creaks o'er the buried caves
  Where the mummied mammoths are.

Then as we linger at luncheon here,
  O'er many a dainty dish,
Let us drink anew to the time when you
  Were a tadpole and I was a fish.

Does Langdon Smith's poem hint at the truth or is it just a fantasy? What do you think?

Glossary

Age regression The use of hypnotism to cause a person in a trance to recall earlier lives.

Akashic Records Memories or records of all events that happened that are imprinted upon a substance of the universe.

Āryas An ancient Sanskrit word meaning "nobles," used by the first Hindus to describe themselves.

Avatar The rebirth of a god on earth to help mankind, according to the Hindu religion.

Brahman The creator spirit of the universe in Hinduism.

Buddha, the THE Buddha is Prince Siddhartha Gautama, founder of the religion Buddhism. A buddha is a person who has attained enlightenment and can enter nirvana.

Cabala Also spelled Kabala and Quabala. Secret Judaic writings of a mystic nature.

Dalai Lama The god-king of Tibetan Buddhism. He is said to be immediately reincarnated upon his death.

Déjà vu   A French term that literally means "seen before." It is a curious feeling that one has seen something or had a particular experience before.

Karma   In both Hinduism and Buddhism karma is the sum of a person's good and bad deeds in a lifetime. Karma controls what one will be born as in the next life.

Kalpa   A very long period of time in Hinduism and Buddhism; over four billion years.

Nirvana   The unexplained place where Buddhist spirits go after escaping the burden of reincarnation.

Origen   Christian priest-writer who believed in reincarnation.

Psychic   A person who is sensitive to the paranormal or supernatural world.

Pyschometry   The belief that a properly psychic person can receive knowledge stored in objects.

Reincarnation   The belief that the human spirit can be reborn in a new body after death.

Samsara   The Wheel of Life, the Hindu word for reincarnation.

Transmigration   Often used as another name for reincarnation, modern authorities say it is more properly used for the rebirth of a human soul into animal or other nonhuman bodies.

Bibliography

Bernstein, Morey, *The Search for Bridey Murphy*. Garden City, N.Y.: Doubleday and Company, 1956.

Bernstein, Morey (with additional material by William J. Barker). *The Search for Bridey Murphy*. Rev. ed. Garden City, N.Y.: Doubleday and Company, 1965.

Cohen, Daniel, *The Mysteries of Reincarnation*. New York: Dodd, Mead and Co., 1975.

Dalai Lama, His Holiness, *My Land and My People*. New York: McGraw-Hill Book Company, 1962.

Ebon, Martin, *Reincarnation in the 20th Century*. New York: World Publishing Co., 1969.

Elbé, Louis, *Future Life*. London: Chatto & Windus, 1907.

Flournoy, Theodore, *From India to the Planet Mars*. Reprinted, New York: University Books, 1963.

Hall, Manly Palmer, *Reincarnation*. Los Angeles: Philosophical Research Society, 1946.

Kelsey, Denys, and Grant, Joan, *Many Lifetimes*. Garden City, N.Y.: Doubleday and Company, 1967.

Langley, Noel, *Edgar Cayce on Reincarnation.* New York: Paperback Library, 1967.

Rato Khyongla Nawang Losang, *My Life and Lives.* New York: E. P. Dutton, 1977.

Ryall, Edward W., *Born Twice.* New York: Harper and Row, 1974.

Stevenson, Dr. Ian, *Twenty Cases Suggestive of Reincarnation.* New York: American Society for Psychical Research, 1966.

Index

145

About the Author

I. G. Edmonds began intensive study of Oriental philosophies and religions while he was stationed in the Far East as a career officer in the United States Air Force. He has also lived in Europe, and has visited such far-flung countries as Ethiopia, Cambodia, and Micronesia. Mr. Edmonds has written more than eighty books for children and adults: *Big U: Universal Pictures in the Silent Days* and *The Mysteries of Troy* are among his recent works. *Other Lives* is his first book for McGraw-Hill. A native of the South, the author now lives in California, where he works as a public-relations manager in the aerospace industry.